MW00966257

TV-free Activities for Kids

by DI HODGES

REDWOOD
EDITIONS

Published by
Redwood Editions
an imprint of
Hinkler Book Distributors Pty. Ltd.
17-23 Redwood Drive
Dingley, Victoria, Australia

ISBN 1 875 980 62 8

Copyright © Hinkler Book Distributors Pty. Ltd. 1998

All rights reserved. This publication is copyright and may not be resold or reproduced in any manner (except excerpt thereof for bona fide study purposes in accordance with the Copyright Act) without the prior consent of the publisher.

This publication is an interactive, educational book designed to teach and entertain children. Some activities will require usage of materials/tools which could cause injury, including serious injury, if swallowed or used. The Publisher, the Editor, or their respective employees or agents, shall not accept responsibility for injury or damage occasioned to any person as a result from participation in any activity in this book, whether or not such injury, loss or damage is in any way due to any negligent act or omission, breach of duty or default on part of the Publisher, the Editor, or their respective employees or agents.

Editor: Gillian Banham
Illustration & Design: Peter Tovey Studio
Production: Tracey Ahern
Publisher: Stephen Ungar

FOREWORD

Do you think your children watch too much TV?

Would you like to spend more quality family time together?

Would you like a year's worth of fantastic, entertaining, learning ideas to share with your children every day?

Then this book is for you!

Like many parents, you probably consider that your children watch too much television. For most families today, television and video-viewing have become an integral part of daily lives, in many cases becoming the only shared activity of the day.

While we all know that television can be a great educational tool, we also know, from countless studies of how children learn, that this is best achieved by 'doing'. The second-hand experiences they gain from watching TV will never replace what children learn through their play and through 'hands on' situations.

Recent research has shown that watching TV has become the most popular recreational activity for children outside school hours. This has contributed to major concerns in our community regarding the high levels of obesity in our children, directly related to sitting down watching TV rather than kicking a ball around or being involved in other active play. Research also suggests that children who watch the most television are the lowest school achievers.

If you would like to replace some of your children's TV viewing time with exciting, creative activities, this book is for you. Most activities are very easily organised from items you will have at home, and they will help develop your children's imaginations and creativity, as well as mental and physical skills.

While some of the activities require adult participation, others only need parents to help the children get started. Don't forget that you are trying to encourage independence, self-confidence and creativity, and it is important to be flexible and let the children decide how things will go. Safety is of the utmost importance though, and supervision with items such as scissors or knives should be closely supervised.

Turn off the TV for an hour a day and spend time with your children. This will help build good communication and understanding, which will stand them in good stead in the years ahead.

ABOUT THE AUTHOR

Di Hodges has been an early childhood teacher for over twenty years. She has taught in a variety of settings, including preschools, prep.classes and Years 1 and 2. She also spent many years helping geographically isolated parents teach their preschoolers at home through the excellent Distance Education facilities offered by Education Queensland. She is currently an Education Adviser (Preschool) with Education Queensland.

Di has a Diploma of Teaching for Early Childhood and Primary, and a Bachelor of Education. She lives on the Gold Coast in Queensland with her husband and preschool son Andrew, and strongly believes that parents are the first and most important teachers of their young children.

Unfortunately, economic pressures on families today often means that parents have to put careers and financial concerns ahead of spending time with their children, and Di hopes this book helps parents and children enjoy playing and learning together again.

Dedication

For my parents, Joan and Stew who have always been there for me, for my husband Geoff for his support, encouragement and ideas and suggestions and, most of all, for my young son Andrew, who has reminded me of the importance of parents in their children's lives.

HOW TO USE THIS BOOK

"**TV Free Activities for Kids**" is full of ideas that you can enjoy trying with your children. Each page contains a short list of materials you will need to collect before you begin the activity. More often than not these are everyday household items you will already have. Save junk (See a Busy Box, *Activity 126*), as many activities in the book use recycled household junk. Other requirements may need to be purchased inexpensively from Newsagents, Craft Shops or your local Dollar Saver-type stores.

The book contains two indexes - an alphabetical one at the end of the book, and a Subject Index at the front. The book is divided into 11 categories -

BRAIN POWER

FOOD FUN

HOME-MADE MUSIC

INDOOR PLAY

LANGUAGE & LITERACY

LET'S CREATE

MATHS IS FUN

OUR ENVIRONMENT

OUTDOOR PLAY

PARTY & GROUP GAMES

SPECIAL OCCASIONS

Each category in the book has activities for children of all ages - from two year olds to older primary children. There will be something that is exactly right for your child. The suggested age on each activity is a guide only - remember that all kids are different and you'll soon know if an activity is too easy or too difficult for your child.

Start with easy ones, give lots of praise and then move onto harder activities.

This book will help you find those areas of learning that your child needs extra time and help with. Don't forget that to succeed at school and in life our children need a healthy self-concept and we parents can foster this with lots of praise, encouragement, time and love. Have fun together!

GUIDE TO SYMBOLS

This simple legend of symbols gives a quick visual reference to the basic elements present in each activity.

Outdoor Activity :
This symbol indicates an outdoor activity.

Indoor Activity :
This symbol indicates an indoor activity.
Note : If both symbols are ticked, the activity can be enjoyed both outdoors and indoors.

Adult Participation : This activity requires some degree of adult supervision. Read the 'What to do' closely to see the degree of monitoring required. This symbol can also indicate participation with an adult is important for learning or sharing.

Pencils, paints and paper : This activity requires the basic drawing or painting tools. It can be as simple as a pencil and paper for keeping score in a game or more art materials for decorating etc.

Tools required : This activity requires tools of some type. This could be anything from a simple bowl and vegetable peeler to balloons and craft materials. All these activities have been designed with the basic everyday items found in the home such as cereal boxes etc. Some activities may require items to be purchased from a shop but should be inexpensive or alternatives can be found. Read the 'What you need' for specific items. Adult supervision is required.

Learning and Imagination : Just about all of the activities in this book encourage imaginative play. There are activities that require some adult participation and may contain important learning skills designed for fun. If the activity is simply a game to occupy a bored child this symbol will not be ticked.

The symbols indicated in this book are a guide only. It is the responsibility of all adults to determine the appropriate activities for each child and the skills they possess. The use of tools requires adult supervision.

symbols

SUBJECT INDEX

An **ALPHABETICAL INDEX** follows the last activity number **365**

BRAIN POWER

AGES   ACTIVITY No.

GREEN DAY

2+

A great way to teach colours to young children.

What You Need

• *Green items - clothing, food, drinks, toys, paint, etc.*

What To Do

Tell your children in the morning that you are going to have a 'Green Day' or whatever colour takes your fancy.   Use your imagination to make it as exciting as you can.
Some possibilities are:

• a small amount of green food colour in their milk:
  'green milk' for their cereal
• a selection of green foods to try:
  honeydew melon
  kiwi fruit
  avocado
  green apple
  snow peas
  celery pieces filled with cream cheese
• select green clothes for you all to wear that day
• do some green cooking:
  avocado dip
  green jelly with chocolate frogs
  green cordial ice blocks
  apple pie
  patty cakes with green icing
• green playdough - make a batch and colour half yellow and half blue
  so they can see it change to green as they play
• add some yellow and blue food colour to their bath water and watch it
  turn green
• be 'greenies' and do lots of gardening - plant some new plants or seeds
• go to a park and collect lots of different leaves for leaf rubbings at
  home with green crayons and pencils
• make some green paint for painting outside
• read 'Green Eggs and Ham' for a bedtime story

activity
1

MAGAZINE PICTURE PUZZLES

Create your own simple jigsaw puzzles with your children from large magazine pictures.

What You Need

- *Large magazine pictures*
- *Glue* • *Scissors*
- *Thick cardboard*

What To Do

Look through magazines with your children and let them choose some pictures from which they would like to make puzzles. Help them cut out the pictures and use a strong glue to stick onto thick cardboard.

When it is dry, cut it into puzzle shapes. With younger children begin with four or five pieces. As they master the skill, cut the pictures into more pieces.

Store and label the puzzles in plastic lunch bags in a shoe box.

activity
2

BOTTLES AND LIDS

4+

This activity will help develop your children's powers of prediction as they guess which lid fits which bottle.   A good way to develop the muscles in their hands and fingers also.

What You Need

• *Bottles of different shapes
  and sizes with screw-top lids.*

What To Do

Put out a selection of jars (at least ten) with lids with different circumferences.   See if your children can find all the correct lids for the jars and screw them on.

Later, they might like to time themselves with an egg-timer to see how fast they can do it.

They could also put the jars in order from the smallest lid to the largest.

(Have your children do this activity on a mat or carpet rather than a hard floor.   Remind them to take great care with glass bottles).

activity
3

BROCHURE MATCHING

A matching activity using junk mail.

4+

What You Need

- *Two matching advertising brochures, magazines or catalogues*
- *Scrap book* • *Scissors* • *Glue*

What To Do

When you next receive some advertising brochures in your mail box ask your neighbours if you can have theirs also when they have finished reading them. (Toy catalogues are great for this activity).

Cut out lots of pictures from one catalogue and paste a picture to each page leaving the opposite page blank.

Give your children the other catalogue to look through. When they find a matching picture, they cut it out and paste it opposite its pair.

activity

4

HOUSEHOLD NOISES

4+ ✓

An excellent listening activity that all the family will enjoy.

 ✓

 ✓

What You Need

- *Tape recorder*
- *Blank tape*

 ✓

 ✓

What To Do

When you have some time on your own, go around the house taping different noises. You might include the bath emptying, the dog chewing a bone, the dishwasher or washing machine, the iron hissing, the postman's bike, the door bell, the vacuum cleaner, the 'phone, the computer and any others you can think of.

Play it back to your children and see how many sounds they can identify. Try out the rest of the family and see how well they listen. I bet that, unfortunately, they are not as familiar with the vacuum cleaner noise as Mum!

activity

5

I WENT SHOPPING

4+

A memory game to play with the rest of the family or some of your children's friends. A good game to play in the car on long trips too!

What You Need

- *A few players*

What To Do

Sit all the players in a circle. The first person says - 'I went shopping and I bought "........" The next player says 'I went shopping and I bought "........" and then says what the first player bought.

Keep going around to see who has the best memory. Vary it by choosing specific shops - 'I went to the toy shop and I bought "........" or 'I went to the fruit shop or newsagents'.

activity

6

MEMORY

4+

A fun way to develop your children's memories.

 ✓

What You Need

 ✓

- *Assortment of small items such as a pencil, rubber, scissors, pen, small toys, hair brush, cutlery etc., tea towel.*
- *Paper and pencil (for older children who are writers)*

 ✓

 ✓

What To Do

 ✓

For younger children select a few items, place on the tray and let your children look at them for a minute. Have your children turn their backs while you remove a couple of items from the tray and cover them with the tea towel. See if your children can tell you what's missing.

For older children place up to 20 items on the tray and cover them up. Uncover them in front of your children and give them a minute to try and memorise, then cover them up again. Your children then write down as many items as possible.

Have a turn yourself and see if your memory is better than your children's. You may be unpleasantly surprised!

activity

7

MISMATCH

4+

A family game to see how observant everyone is.

 ✓

What You Need

• *Two or more players*

What To Do

 ✓

If the whole family plays, divide into two teams. If just a few play, one person at a time can have a turn.

The first player or team leaves the room. The other team or players mismatch five things around the room - perhaps put some cushions on the floor instead of the couch, turn an ornament upside down, put someone's shoes on their hands instead of feet, or a t-shirt on inside out. I am sure you will think of heaps to do.

When the player or team returns, they have to spot the five mismatches. For any they do not notice, the other player or team score a point.

The next player or team then has a turn. The player or team with the most points is the winner.

activity
8

NUTS AND BOLTS

4+

Another thinking ahead and predicting activity. This game will also help your children learn how to screw and unscrew bolts - great for developing the hand and finger muscles needed for writing.

What You Need

• *A selection of different sized screws with nuts they will screw into.*

What To Do

Give your children at least a dozen different sized bolts and matching nuts.   See if they can find the ones that go together and screw the nuts into the bolts.

To increase the challenge they might like to:
• beat the clock - time them and see if they can beat their PB (personal best)
• beat an egg-timer
• do it blind-folded
• time each other or another family member and see who is the fastest

activity
9

ODD ONE OUT

4+

Help your younger children begin to understand the meaning of same and different.

What You Need

- *Sets of objects that have two exactly the same, e.g.*
- *Pair of socks*
- *Pair of shoes*
- *2 matching mugs*
- *2 matching forks*

What To Do

Mix up the items and have your children find the two that are exactly the same. Then they cover their eyes. Put a pair of objects together with one that is different. They have to find the odd one out and tell you why it doesn't belong.

Make this game more and more difficult by making the differences more and more subtle.

activity
10

QUERIES

4+

Pose some simple 'queries', for your children to solve! Activities like this increase their reasoning capacity and make them better at problem solving.

What You Need

• *time together*

What To Do

Pose questions to your children like - 'I'm thinking of something that jingles and jangles and we need them to open the door?'
~ Keys
'I'm thinking of something you can pedal that has three wheels'
~ A tricycle
'I'm thinking of something that's pretty to look at, smells sweet and grows in a garden.' ~ Flowers
'I'm thinking of something we can make out of detergent, that sails in the air, and then goes pop' ~ Bubbles
'I'm thinking of something you like to lick that's cold and sweet.'
~ An ice-cream or iceblock.
'I'm thinking of someone who loves you lots and who you love to visit.'
~ Nana
'I'm thinking of something you put up in the rain to stay dry.'
~ An umbrella
'I'm thinking of something that's colourful and soft and you like to throw and catch it.' ~ A ball

As your children gain mastery at 'queries', make the questions harder and harder. Perhaps they would like to pose some for you.

activity

11

WHO'S MISSING?

A game to develop thinking skills.

4+

What You Need

• *A group of children*

What To Do

A great game to play with a group of children at a birthday party or any sort of gathering. The children sit in a circle and one child is sent away where they cannot see or hear what is happening.

Another child is chosen from the group to go and hide out of sight. Make sure that all the remaining children are certain who is hiding. Then, the first child is allowed to return, and looks around the circle to try to remember who is missing. If they cannot remember, the other children can offer clues! Perhaps something the hidden child is wearing or perhaps the first letter of their name. Allow three clues only. If the first child has not guessed, the hidden child comes out of hiding and the game starts all over again with two more children.

activity

12

DOTS AND DASHES

6+

A game of skill to play with your children.

What You Need

• *Two players* • *Pencils* • *Paper*

What To Do

Draw lots of rows of dots on the paper first. The number of dots you draw will determine how long the game will last.

The players now take it in turns to draw a line connecting one dot to another. You can draw the lines any direction but diagonally. The aim of the game is to form squares between four of the dots.

The person who draws the last line which forms a square 'owns' that square and writes their initial in it. They then have another turn.

If a single line makes two squares, that player 'owns' both squares but only gets one more turn. Help your children with the strategies of the game so they understand not to make it too easy for their opponent.

At the end, tally up the squares to see who is the winner.

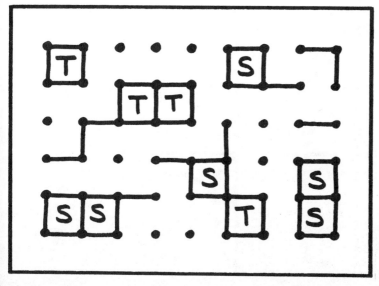

activity

13

Os and Xs (sometimes called Tic-Tac-Toe) 6+

A simple game of strategy.

What You Need

- *Two players*
- *Paper*
- *2 pencils*

What To Do

Show your children how to draw two horizontal parallel lines crossed by two vertical parallel lines to make nine spaces in three rows.

One player draws the Xs and the other the Os. The first player to get three Xs or three Os in a row in any direction is the winner.

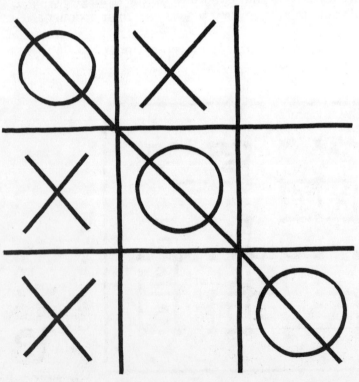

activity

14

SLAP JACK

6+

A great card game to play with your children and a way to introduce the four suits in a pack of cards.

What You Need

- *A pack of playing cards*
- *2 or more players*

What To Do

The aim of this game is to collect the whole fifty-two cards in the pack.

Deal out the whole pack one at a time to the players. The cards are dealt face down and the players don't look at their cards.

Take it in turns to put a card on a pile in the middle. If a Jack is turned up the first player to slap the Jack takes all the cards in the middle.

Players must place the cards in the middle without looking at them first and turning the card and slapping must be done with the same hand.

If a player slaps a card that is not a Jack, they must pay a penalty and give a card from the bottom of their pack to all the other players.

For a variation you can play 'Slap Fiver' or 'Slap Acer'.

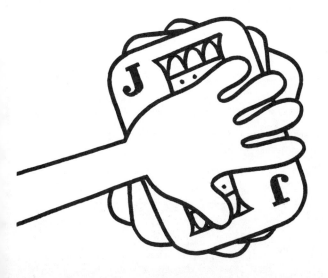

activity
15

FOOD FUN

BANANA PANCAKES

2+

 ✓
 ✓

Nutritionists tell us that we all should eat a banana a day. When you have some extra-ripe bananas in the house, help your children make some Banana Pancakes for a healthy snack.

 ✓
 ✓

What You Need

- *2 ripe bananas*
- *1 egg*
- *1 cup of self-raising flour (use wholemeal if you wish)*
- *3/4 cup of milk*
- *1 tablespoon of butter*

What To Do

The children can help with the first step of mashing the bananas well. Next let one of them break the egg and whisk well into the bananas until smooth and creamy. Next measure in the flour and 1/2 of the milk and beat for 1 minute with a large spoon. Stir in the rest of the milk.

Cover the mixture with a tea-towel and allow it to stand for about half an hour.

In a frypan add a teaspoon of butter and pour or ladle in some of the mixture to form small pancakes.

When bubbles appear on the side turn carefully with an egg lifter and cook until golden brown on the other side. Banana Pancakes are delicious served warm with icecream and sliced bananas for dessert or cold for a snack. Makes about 12.

activity

16

BUTTERFLY SANDWICHES 2+

Even the pickiest eater in your family will love these sandwiches, especially if they helped in the making.

 ✓

 ✓

What You Need

- *bread*
- *cream cheese, cheese, peanut paste or Vegemite*
- *decorations such as fruit or vegetable pieces, cheese slices, slices of sausage or ham, gherkins, celery, sultanas or anything else tasty and colourful.*

 ✓

 ✓

What To Do

Stand your children on a chair beside you at the kitchen bench so they can help. Cut a slice of bread into either two or four triangles and face them outwards on a plate to form the 'butterflies.' Apply a spread to the triangles, then decorate - your children will love helping with this part and making suggestions. Cheese slices cut up with celery pieces are yummy on Vegemite, or banana rings and sultanas on peanut paste are just great. Use strips of carrots, beans, or capsicums for antennae. Yum! Yum!

activity
17

CHEERIO KEBABS

2+

Cheerios are also called cocktail sausages. Children love them though, like most parents, I consider them party fare. However they will enjoy helping you make them into exciting kebabs for their own dinner or for a special occasion such as a birthday party or a sausage sizzle with friends.

What You Need

- *1 kg of cheerios*
- *cherry tomatoes*
- *diced cucumber*
- *large can pineapple pieces*
- *can of baby corn cobs*
- *stuffed olives (if your children like them)*

MARINADE INGREDIENTS
- *1 tablespoon lemon juice*
- *1 tablespoon of brown sugar*
- *2 teaspoons of French mustaad*
- *Reserved pineapple syrup*

What To Do

Make the marinade by combining the pineapple syrup, brown sugar, mustard and lemon juice in a saucepan. Bring the mixture to the boil and boil until it is reduced to a third.

The children can help by dicing the cucumber, cutting the cheerios in half and putting the other ingredients into dishes. Then they will have lots of fun threading their own kebab sticks. (if you soak the wooden skewers or kebab sticks overnight they will be less likely to burn on the grill or bar-b-que). Use a pastry brush to brush their finished kebabs with the marinade mixture and baste some more as they are cooking. Yum! Any that are left are delicious cold in your children's school lunch boxes.

activity
18

CHOCCY BANANA ICEBLOCKS 2+

Children love bananas and they are very good for them when you have a lot to use up. Try this delicious recipe.

What You Need

- *Bananas*
- *Cooking chocolate*
- *Paddle pop sticks*

What To Do

Your children can help by peeling the bananas and the older ones can cut the bananas in half across. Poke a paddle-pop stick into the end of each banana, then place them on a tray and freeze.

When they are frozen dip them in the melted chocolate. Very yummy!

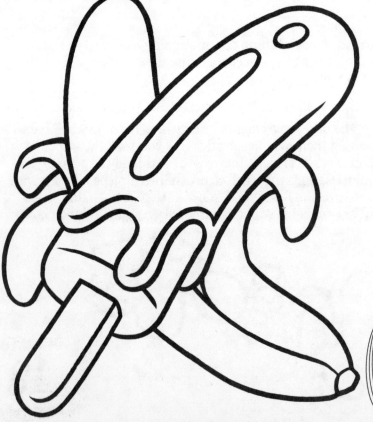

activity

19

CHOCOLATE CRACKLES

2+

A yummy treat to make with your children for special occasions.

 ✓

 ✓

What You Need

- *4 cups of Rice Bubbles*
- *3 tablespoons of cocoa*
- *1 and 1/2 cups of icing sugar*
- *1 cup of coconut*
- *250g of Cophaa*

 ✓

What To Do

Your children will enjoy sifting the icing sugar into a large mixing bowl. Next they can measure and add the other dry ingredients. They can then mix these well. Meanwhile, melt the copha gently in a saucepan and cool a little. Carefully pour the copha into the bowl of dry ingredients. Be careful that the children are safely away as you do this. When the mixture has cooled enough to handle they will love filling patty cases with the mixture. Cool on a tray in the refrigerator and enjoy!

activity **20**

EGG FLIP

2+

 ✓

 ✓

Whenever my child is off his food, an egg flip is something I can always get into him. What's more, he likes to help me make it too!

What You Need

Ingredients
- *1 egg* • *Milk* • *Sugar* • *Nutmeg*
- *Vanilla essence*
- *(sometimes I add a banana also)*

 ✓

What To Do

Your children can help you collect all the ingredients and utensils, then they can break the egg into the bowl, add the vanilla and two teaspoons of sugar. Hold the bowl while they beat the mixture until it is frothy. Next, they pour in one cup of milk and then beat it again.

Help them pour the egg flip into a glass and sprinkle the top with a little nutmeg.

activity **21**

FRENCH TOAST

2+

A yummy breakfast that is easy to cook together.

What You Need

Ingredients
- *1 egg*
- *1/2 cup milk*
- *2 teaspooons butter*
- *4 slices of bread*
- *Honey, golden or maple syrup*

What To Do

Collect all the utensils and ingredients together. Help your children crack the egg and then they can beat it and add the milk. Mix well. Melt the butter in a fry pan and, when it is bubbling, dip two slices of bread in the egg and milk mixture and cook. Turn once.

Serve warm with honey, golden syrup or maple syrup. We like it with maple syrup best - a favourite Sunday morning breakfast in our house.

activity

22

FRUIT KEBABS

2+

Make eating fruit an exciting experience for your children by showing them how to thread fruit kebabs.

 ✓

 ✓

What You Need

A selection of fruits in season - have your children help prepare them - perhaps melon balls, chunks of bananas, strawberries, orange or mandarin segments, slices of kiwi fruit, chunks of apple and so on.

 ✓

What To Do

After your children have helped you prepare the fruit, put the fruit on a large platter, provide them with kebab sticks and let them thread on their own selection. Make sure they eat the fruit from the side of the sticks so they don't spike their mouths. Children love the novelty of this and even those who are not keen on fruit will enjoy it prepared this way.

activity

23

FRUIT SMOOTHIES

2+

 ✓
 ✓

 ✓

A great way to get fruit and milk into reluctant eaters.

What You Need

- *1/2 cup cold milk*
  (children should always have full-cream milk)
- *6 strawberries or 1 banana or any other fruit*
  you may have that will blend well
- *1/4 cup flavoured yoghurt*

What To Do

Your children will enjoy helping you measure in all the ingredients. Blend well until nice and frothy. Pour into a tall glass, add a straw and watch it disappear! Makes enough for one serve.

activity
24

FUNNY EGG FACES

2+

 ✓
 ✓

 ✓
 ✓

Sometimes we have to resort to clever trickery to encourage our children to eat healthy food. Your children will love to help you make these funny egg faces and hopefully will enjoy eating them at the end.

What You Need

- *Boiled eggs*
- *Grated cheese, carrot or shredded lettuce for 'hair'*
- *Sultanas, pieces of tomato or beetroot for the facial features*
- *Mayonnaise or cream cheese for the adhesive*

What To Do

Help your children cut their egg in half and place the halves on a plate. They then use their imagination to make hair and facial features on their egg. Make a body with triangles or rectangles of buttered bread. Then they get to eat their creation!

Another alternative is to make a clown by cutting off the top of the egg and keeping it for the hat. Carefully scoop out the yolk and mix it with a little tomato sauce or perhaps some salmon and lemon juice, or mayonnaise. Pile the filling back into the egg and place the top back on to make the clown's hat. Tiny pieces of tomato or capsicum could make the face. Sit the clown on some shredded lettuce 'grass.'

activity
25

ALPHABET BIKKIES 4+

Help your young children learn their letters by making some Alphabet Bikkies together.

What You Need

- *1 cup of self raising flour*
- *1/2 tablespoon of cornflour*
- *1/3 cup butter or margarine*
- *1/4 cup castor sugar*
- *1 beaten egg*

What To Do

Your children will be able to help with lots in this simple dough recipe. Begin by helping them sift the flour and cornflour into a mixing bowl. Next show them how to rub in the butter. Last of all they can help break the egg into a small bowl and beat it with a fork or whisk. Add the mixture with the sugar. Next lightly flour a board and with their hands they can knead the dough until it's pliable. Break it into small pieces and they can roll it into little sausages. Help them shape the dough sausages into the letters of their name. Perhaps they know how to spell some other words - Mum or Dad, or perhaps the names of their brothers or sisters. Ask if there are any other letters they would like to make and show them how to make them. 'Mum, can we make the letter that Bandy-dog's name starts with?', or 'Mum, what letter does Nanny start with, or Pa?'

Bake the letters in a moderate oven (180°C) for about 20 minutes and cool on a rack. They are delicious plain or you might like to help the children ice them when they have cooled. Ours never last long enough to be iced! Makes about 12.

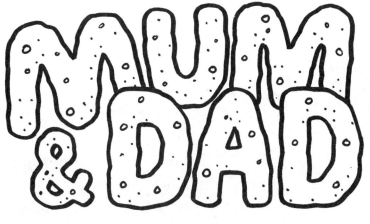

activity
26

BANANA DATE SQUARES 4+

A healthy snack your children will love helping you make, and all the family will love eating!

What You Need

Ingredients
- *3 bananas*
- *1 cup dates*
- *1/2 cup pecan nuts*
- *1/3 cup cooking oil*
- *2 cups rolled oats*
- *1 teaspoon vanilla essence*
- *1/2 teaspoon salt*

What To Do

Your children can help collect all the utensils and ingredients. Older children will also be able to chop the dates and pecans. Younger children can help with the measuring, pouring and mashing.

Your children can peel and mash the bananas in the bowl. Next add the chopped dates, nuts and oil and mix well. Add the vanilla, rolled oats and salt and again mix well. Let the mixture stand for 5 minutes so the oats absorb the moisture.

Push into a greased baking tray and bake for 25 minutes at 180°C.

Cut into squares while still warm. Yummy but still healthy.

activity
27

BUTTER CHURNS

4+

Show your children how butter was made in the olden days with this simple butter churn.

 ✓

What You Need

 ✓

- *250ml of pure whipping cream*
- *jar or plastic container with a secure lid*
- *1 marble*

 ✓

What To Do

 ✓

Pour the cream into the container and add the marble. Take turns with the children to shake the container (not too hard!) After about ten minutes the cream should have changed into butter. Taste the left-over butter milk. Compare the butter you have made with commercially made butter you have in the 'fridge. Can the children see and taste any difference? Explain how the butter was traditionally made into small pats and often printed with a simple design.

Make some bread and butter sandwiches with the butter you have made together.

activity
28

DOUGH SCULPTURES

4+

 ✓
 ✓

 ✓
 ✓

Make delicious dough creations that you and your children can really eat. Yum! Yum!

What You Need

- *1 packet yeast* • *300 mls warm water*
- *1 teaspoon salt* • *1 tablespoon sugar*
- *4 cups plain flour* • *1 egg (beaten)*

What To Do

Help your children measure the warm water and pour into a large bowl. They can then sprinkle on the yeast and stir it until it is soft.

Next, they can help measure and then add the salt, sugar and flour. Mix into a dough and form a ball.

Show your children how to knead the dough until it is smooth and pliable. They can then shape the dough into shapes, letters, animals and whatever takes their fancy. Put the shapes onto a greased baking tray and cover with a tea towel. Leave in a warm spot until they have risen to double in size.

Next, your children can 'paint' their shapes with the beaten egg and bake in a moderate oven for 10-15 minutes until the bread creations are golden brown.

They'll look almost too good to eat!

activity
29

GEOMETRIC SHAPE SANDWICHES 4+

Teach your young children their geometric shapes in a yummy edible way!

What You Need

- *Sliced bread*
- *Fillings such as egg and lettuce, cheese slices, ham, peanut paste and any other favourites.*

What To Do

Your children will enjoy helping make the sandwich fillings. This is a great opportunity to introduce new taste sensations to them such as peanut paste and sultanas or avocado and sprouts.

After the sandwiches are made, help the children to carefully cut them into different shapes - triangles, rectangles, squares and use a scone cutter to make circles.

Take them outside on a rug in the garden with a large jug of juice and enjoy a shape picnic together.

activity
30

GINGERBREAD MEN

4+

 ✓

Read or tell the story of the Gingerbread Man to your children and then make some together.

 ✓

What You Need
- *1 cup of plain flour*
- *1/2 cup of sugar*
- *125 grams of butter*
- *1 egg*
- *1/2 teaspoon of baking soda*
- *2 teaspoons of ground ginger*
- *Mixed fruit for decoration*

 ✓

 ✓

What To Do

The children will love helping find all the necessary utensils and ingredients for the recipe and of course helping with the measuring.

Cream the sugar and butter, then add the egg and beat well. Let them help use the flour sifter to sift the flour and then add the baking soda and ginger.

Using a floured roller, roll out the gingerbread on a floured board. The children will love to help cut out their gingerbread men and then help them lift them with a lifter onto a greased oven tray.

Now for the fun stuff! Give them mixed fruit or even chocolate bits to decorate their gingerbread men. Perhaps a cherry nose, sultana eyes, some peel for the mouth and currant or chocolate buttons.

Cook the gingerbread men in a moderate oven for 15-20 minutes.

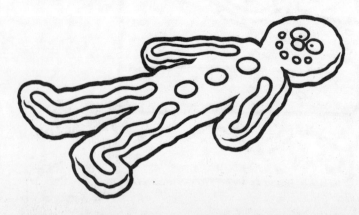

activity
31

HEALTHY APRICOT TREATS

4+

A yummy and easy recipe that's also healthy for them.

What You Need

- *1 cup of chopped dried apricots*
- *1/2 cup of orange juice*
- *4 tablespoons of honey*
- *1 cup of powdered milk*
- *1/2 cup of desiccated coconut*

What To Do

Simmer the apricots, orange juice and the honey in a saucepan for about 10 minutes. Add the powdered milk to the mixture. Pour into a mixing bowl and mix well. Chill in the fridge until cool.

Later your children will enjoy rolling the mixture into balls and coating them with coconut.

Store in the 'fridge - but they won't last long. Makes about 24.

activity

32

HOME-MADE LEMONADE

4+

An easy drink recipe your children will enjoy making with you to share with the rest of the family.

What You Need

- 4 lemons
- 1/2 cup sugar or honey
- 1/2 cup of hot water
- 4 cups of cold water
- Ice cubes
- Lemon squeezer
- Large jug

What To Do

Ask your children to count out four lemons. Help them cut the lemons in half and they can then juice them with a juicer. (We have an electric juicer and my son loves making lemon and orange juice with it). Pour the juice into a large jug.

Your children can measure out the honey or sugar, but add the hot water to dissolve it yourself.

Next your children pour out and add to the jug the four cups of cold water. Add the honey or sugar solution and let them stir well.

Add some lemon slices and a tray of ice cubes for a decorative touch.

For a slightly fizzy lemonade you can substitute a bottle of spritzig mineral water or soda water for the plain cold water.

activity
33

HONEY AND ORANGE WHIP   4+

Make a delicious and healthy drink for the whole family on a hot day. This drink is also delicious poured into iceblock containers and frozen.

What You Need

- *1 dozen oranges or a bottle of commercial orange juice and 3 oranges*
- *1/4 cup of honey*

What To Do

Cut the oranges and help your children squeeze them in a juicer to make six cups of orange juice. My four year old loves using our electric juicer to make orange juice for breakfast. Next peel the oranges and help them cut the oranges into segments, making sure you remove all the pips. Combine the orange juice, oranges, and honey and blend in a couple of batches until smooth.

This recipe makes about ten cups. Drink some now and freeze some for yummy good-for-them iceblocks later! Makes 4 glasses.

activity
34

JUNKET

Junket is a yummy, healthy dessert that your young children will enjoy helping you make. We always loved it as children - try it with your own kids.

 ✓

 ✓

What You Need

- *1 junket tablet (Junket tablets are sold in packets in your supermarket)*
- *1 and 1/2 cups of milk*
- *2 teaspoons of sugar*
- *food colouring*
- *nutmeg, coconut or sprinkles*

 ✓

 ✓

What To Do

Your children will enjoy watching the junket tablet dissolve in a teaspoon of water. Meanwhile, heat the milk in a saucepan - only until blood heat - the junket will not set if the milk is too hot. Stir the dissolved tablet into the milk. Your children can add a few drops of food colouring if they like. Pour the junket into serving bowls. Adults like nutmeg or coconut sprinkled on the top but my bet is the children will want colourful sprinkles or hundreds and thousands.

The junket needs a few hours in the 'fridge to become quite cold before serving. Makes four servings.

activity
35

PARFAITS

4+

 ✓

 ✓

 ✓

 ✓

The whole family will love assembling (and eating) their delicious parfait desserts. They are traditionally made in tall parfait glasses but any long glasses will be fine. However, you will need spoons with long handles to reach all the delicious dessert at the bottom!

What You Need

- *A variety of fillings for the parfaits
  - the children can help prepare them.*
- *Fruit - fruit salad works well or any
  tinned or fresh fruit chopped well*
- *Jelly - make up a jelly with the children
  in their favourite flavour*
- *Custard - make your own or buy a commercially made one*
- *Whipped cream*
- *Crushed nuts and wafer biscuits for the top*

What To Do

Set out the glasses and the fillings and let the family layer their own parfaits. They look great with contrasting layers of colour. Top with some toasted or crushed nuts and wafer triangles. They'll be coming back for more!

activity
36

PIKELET LETTERS

4+

Cooking with children involves many learning areas - reading recipes together, following directions and measuring. As well making letter pikelets helps them learn the alphabet in a really fun way!

 ✓

 ✓

What You Need

• *A basic pikelet recipe*

 ✓

What To Do

 ✓

Don't forget to involve your children in making the mixture - children always eat more if they have helped in the cooking process.

Make your pikelet batter in a jug for easy pouring. Carefully pour the batter into a hot greased pan in the shape of individual letters. Once the letters begin to bubble you can pour a little more batter onto the top of the letter to form traditional round pikelets and the letter section will stand out in relief when you turn it.

Otherwise just leave the letter shapes and turn them carefully. Your children will have great fun making their name as well as other words, and even more fun eating them!

activity
37

PIZZA

4+

A guaranteed culinary success with all the family.

What You Need

Ingredients
- *Pita bread or pizza bases*
- *Bacon*
- *Cheese*
- *Mild salami sausage*
- *Tomato paste or pizza paste*
- *Vegetables such as zucchini, capsicum, mushrooms, onion, pineapple*

What To Do

Place the pizza base on a baking tray and your children can spread the tomato paste over it.   Next, they grate the cheese and sprinkle that over the tomato paste.

Together, cut up the bacon and vegetables and sprinkle over the cheese.

Cook in a hot oven for 15-20 minutes.

activity
38

SANDWICH SMORGASBORD 4+

This idea came from the Dental Therapists in the School Dental Unit attached to the school where I teach. They organise a wonderful 'Taste Testing for Preschoolers' where the children are encouraged to try new, healthy taste sensations. As a mother I find it very disheartening when my child refuses to try new foods. However, I have found that if he is involved in the food preparation he is more likely to try something different. You could try this with just your own children or when you next have a few others over to play for the day.

What You Need

A variety of breads, fillings and spreads. A selection of bread could include pita bread, cruskits, wholemeal bread or perhaps foccacia. The fillings could include cold meats or chicken, salmon, salad items such as grated carrots, shredded lettuce, alfalfa sprouts, thin strips of beetroot and grated cheese. The spreads could include old favourites such as Vegemite and peanut paste as well as new taste sensations such as cream cheese, ricotta cheese, mashed avocado or hommus. Make sure the kids are involved in the preparation of all this.

What To Do

When the food is all prepared, set it out attractively with jugs of cold water and juice and cups and plates. The children help themselves and make exotic sandwiches. Encourage them to try new combinations. After they have finished they might like to draw what they had and make it into a recipe book for future 'Sandwich Smorgasbords.' Talk about what worked well together and what was 'yucky.'

A great idea for a picnic also.

activity

39

SESAME SNAPS

4+

A healthy, chewy snack that children adore.

 ✓

 ✓

 ✓

What You Need

Ingredients
- 3/4 cup honey
- 1/2 cup sunflower seeds
- 1/2 cup skim milk powder
- 1 cup sesame seeds
- 1/2 cup shredded coconut

Utensils
- Measuring cup
- Large saucepan
- Mixing spoon
- Flat dish or baking tray

What To Do

Your children can help collect the ingredients and utensils needed for this recipe.

Bring the honey to the boil and then add all the other ingredients. Your children can help measure them, but you will have to do the pouring and mixing.

Pour the mixture into a flat dish and pop it into the 'fridge to set. When it's cold, slice into rectangles.

activity
40

SHAKE UP THE MILO

4+

Help your children learn how to make a yummy milk shake for themselves.

 ✓

What You Need

 ✓

Ingredients
- *Milo*
- *Milk*
- *Ice cream*
- *Hot water*

Utensils
- *Teaspoon*
- *Glass*
- *Plastic beaker with lid*

✓

What To Do

Your children can measure two teaspoons of Milo into the beaker. Add a little hot water yourself, but they can mix it well to dissolve the Milo.

Next, they pour out a glass of milk and add that to the beaker with a big spoonful of ice cream. Help them put the lid firmly on the beaker and they can shake it vigorously.

Let them pour it into a glass and enjoy!

activity
41

SOUP FOR LUNCH

4+

 ✓

 ✓

Most children love soup and they will love this tasty, healthy soup even more because they have helped to make it. Bon appetit!

What You Need

 ✓

- *Mixture of vegetables such as a carrot, a couple of celery stalks, a potato, peas in the pod, beans, a tomato, a parsnip and a zucchini*
- *Bacon or ham pieces*

 ✓

- *olive oil*
- *stock cube*
- *dry pasta*
- *vegetable peeler*
- *vegetable knife*
- *large soup pot*

What To Do

Involve your children as much as possible in preparing the soup, letting them peel the potato, scrape the carrot with the vegie peeler, shell the peas and so on.

Cook the bacon or ham in a little oil and your children will be able to then tip in the prepared vegetables carefully. Add some water, the stock cube and about 1/2 a cup of dried pasta. Bring the soup to the boil and then let it simmer for about 30 minutes. Delicious served with crusty bread or toast fingers. Your children will enjoy the accolades of the whole family! Makes enough for 6.

activity
42

VEGETABLE TASTING

4+

Cooking together can help picky eaters develop an interest in food and try something new.

 ✓

 ✓

What You Need

- *Selection of raw vegetables*
- *Vegetable peeler*
- *Bowl of cold water*
- *Cutting board*

 ✓

What To Do

Many parents complain that their young children won't eat vegetables but I have always found at preschool that they prefer raw vegies to cooked ones. Involve your young children in the shopping and preparation of a raw vegetable platter and I'm sure you will be surprised!

There is rarely a meal prepared at our home where my three year old is not standing on a chair beside me at the kitchen bench 'helping'. I am hoping that this early interest in food preparation will make him a better cook than his Dad!

Put your children up beside you and they can help wash the vegetables, peel cucumber and carrots and help break up vegetables such as cauliflower or broccoli. Older children can use a small sharp knife but always supervise carefully.

Vegetables can taste delicious on their own or even more interesting with a dipping sauce, Avocado Dip is usually popular, or just tomato or a mild soy sauce, mild sweet and sour or a packet of French Onion soup mixed with sour cream or yoghurt. Your child will be able to make up these simple sauces also.

Next time your children have friends to play help them make up a vegie platter and dipping sauce before the friends arrive and watch it disappear.

activity
43

CHEESEY BALLS

6+

A delicious, easy, savoury treat you can make with the children.

What You Need

- *1 tablespoon butter*
- *1 and 1/2 cups of self raising flour*
- *1 cup instant oats*
- *1 cup milk*
- *1 cup of grated Cheddar cheese*

What To Do

Show the children how to rub the butter into the flour until it resembles crumbs. Next they can grate the cheese and add it to the flour and butter mixture. Then add the oats and milk and mix well. They'll enjoy rolling the mixture into small balls. Place them on a well greased scone tray and bake at 200ºC for 10-15 minutes until golden brown. Delicious warm but also great cold. Makes about 15.

activity

44

FRIED RICE

A healthy tea to cook with your children that all the family will enjoy.

 ✓
 ✓

 ✓
 ✓

What You Need

Ingredients:
- *1.5 cups rice* • *Water*
- *1 onion* • *2 eggs*
- *4 bacon rashers or ham*
- *Frozen peas* • *Other vegetables the family likes: e.g. corn, capsicum, etc*
- *Soya sauce*
- *Oil for cooking*

What To Do

Bring about six cups of water to the boil and add the rice. When it is cooked, pour into a colander, let it drain and cool. Your children will be interested in the difference between a cooked and uncooked grain of rice.

Then they can help you chop up the onion, bacon and any other vegies you want to add.

Add some oil to a pan and cook the onion and bacon, then remove.

Let your children break the eggs carefully into a bowl and mix together with a fork. Pour into the fry pan and let it cook like an omelette. Cut into pieces and add the cooked rice, bacon, onion and the rest of the ingredients. Mix together and all enjoy.

I find my child (who is a fairly picky eater, like most three year olds) really enjoys eating the meals he has helped to prepare.

activity
45

JELLY FRUIT FLUMMERY

6+

I don't know where the word 'flummery' comes from but children love these delicious fluffy desserts, especially if they have helped make them.

What You Need

- *1 packet of jelly crystals in your children's favourite flavour*
- *1/2 cup of castor sugar*
- *fruit - chopped bananas, pineapple or kiwi fruit pieces or passionfruit pulp.*
- *1 egg*
- *1 cup of milk*

What To Do

Your children can help stir the jelly crystals in one cup of hot water to dissolve them thoroughly. Stand the jelly until it's cool but not set. Add one cup of cold water from the 'fridge. Let your children beat the egg with the sugar until nice and frothy and then add the milk. Help them cut up the fruit and add to the jelly mixture. Then add the beaten mixture, stirring thoroughly together. Put the jelly fruit flummery into a pretty bowl and put into the 'fridge to set. A favourite dessert for young and old at our place. Makes enough for six.

activity
46

MALTY BALLS

6+

A delicious and healthy snack to make together.

 ✓

 ✓

What You Need

Ingredients:
- *1 cup skim milk powder*
- *1/2 cup powdered milk*
- *2 cups corn flakes*
- *1/2 cup sultanas*
- *1/4 cup coconut*
- *1 teaspoon carob or cocoa*
- *1/2 teaspoon vanilla*
- *Water or fruit juice to bind*

 ✓

What To Do

Combine all the dry ingredients in a large bowl. Gradually add enough water or juice to combine.

Your children will enjoy rolling teaspoonfuls of the mixture in extra coconut. Keep them chilled.

Great for a picnic or a healthy snack at home.

activity
47

POTATO PRINTS

6+

Children of all ages love printing and you can use their colourful prints for wrapping paper.

What You Need

- *potatoes*
- *small, sharp kitchen knife*
- *thin felt pen*
- *styrofoam trays*
- *paint made from food colouring and wall paper paste or commercial paint*

- *lots of newspaper*
- *paper or card*
- *kitchen sponges*

What To Do

Cut the potatoes in half and suggest to your children that they draw some simple design with the thin felt pen on the potato halves. Next cut carefully around the shapes for them. Older children may be able to do this for themselves.

Put the kitchen sponges on the styrofoam trays and pour a little paint on each - a different colour on each one.

Put plenty of newspaper on a flat working surface and show them how to print by pushing down firmly on the sponge and then printing on their paper. If you have some cardboard, they could print some cards. Keep them for use in the future. The printed paper makes excellent wrapping paper and everyone will be impressed by the children's creativity.

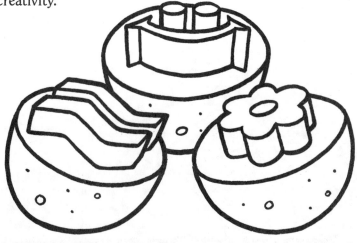

activity
48

CHRISTMAS RUM BALLS

8+

Make some Rum Balls with your children for the family or to give as gifts at Christmas time. Great for your children's teachers, the neighbours - our milkman even got some last year! Here's an easy but delicious recipe your older children can make on their own.

What You Need

- *9 Vita Brits • 1 can condensed milk*
- *2 dessertspoons cocoa*
- *1/2 cup dessicated coconut*
- *1/2 cup minced or finely chopped sultanas*
- *2 tablespoons rum*
- *Extra coconut or chocolate hundreds & thousands for rolling*

What To Do

In a large bowl, your children crush the Vita Brits with their hands or a rolling pin. Add all the other ingredients. The sultanas are best minced in a mincer (about the only time I use mine) or they can be finely chopped - you will have to help with this step.

Mix very well. Your children then roll teaspoonsfuls in their clean hands (make hand-washing a prerequisite for cooking). Then they roll the ball in the extra coconut or chocolate hundreds and thousands.

The Rum Balls make a decorative gift wrapped in cellophane and tied with Christmas ribbon.

activity
49

COCONUT MACAROONS   8+

Older children will love making these yummy bikkies and the whole family will love eating them.

What You Need

- 2 cups of desiccated coconut
- 1 cup of castor sugar
- 2 tablespoons of cornflour
- pinch of salt
- 2 eggs

What To Do

First your children measure all the dry ingredients into a mixing bowl. Next they beat the eggs well and add to the dry ingredients. Mix them together well. Grease your biscuit trays and cover with Glad Bake as macaroons tend to stick to the tray.

Place teaspoonfuls onto the trays, leaving room for the macaroons to spread.

Bake in a slow oven - 150°C - for about 15 to 20 minutes.

Makes about 24.

activity
50

POTATO FRITTERS

8+

A favourite recipe from my childhood that your children will enjoy helping to make and eat!

What You Need

- *3 medium sized potatoes*
- *2 beaten eggs*
- *1/2 cup of plain flour*
- *1/2 teaspoonful of salt*

What To Do

Peel the potatoes and your children will enjoy grating them into a colander. Rinse and squeeze out the excess liquid. Next they will enjoy breaking the eggs into a mixing bowl and beating them with a fork or whisk. Add the potatoes to the eggs and then the flour and salt. Let the children mix them well. Shape into fritters. Add a small amount of cooking oil to a hot frypan and cook until golden brown. Makes 10-15.

activity

51

BAKED APPLES

10+

A yummy dessert your older children will enjoy making (with a little adult help) for the whole family.

What You Need

I'll give the quantities for one apple - it's a good maths lesson for your children to work out how much is needed for an apple per family member.

- *1 Granny Smith cooking apple*
- *1 teaspoon of crushed nuts* • *1/2 teaspoon coconut*
- *1/2 teaspoon sultanas*   • *1 tablespoon honey*

What To Do

Wash the apple and carefully core it with an apple corer, making sure you don't make the hole go through to the other side or all the delicious filling will dribble out. Fill the centre with the crushed nuts, sultanas and coconut. (If you are making the apple for children under 5 it's best to leave out the crushed nuts in case they choke).

Next, your children can dribble the honey over the sides and into the centre of the apple. Bake the apples on a tray or in an oven-proof dish for about 45 minutes at 200ºC.

Delicious served with ice-cream.

activity
52

SAUCY MEATLOAF

10+

Most children want to cook and, although it is often quicker to cook on your own, it is very important that you let them try. Think how great it will be when they are older and can take over and give you a night off! My sister and I used to love cooking on Sunday afternoons when our parents played tennis. When we were young we went with them but as older teenagers we often stayed home and cooked Sunday night dinner. Older children will be able to do most of this recipe on their own.

What You Need

- *500g sausage mince* } *or use 1 kg of minced*
- *500g minced steak* } *steak if preferred*
- *1 cup of fresh breadcrumbs*
- *2 onions, finely chopped*   • *1/2 cup of milk*
- *2 teaspoons of curry powder* • *1/2 cup of water*
- *salt and pepper*   • *chopped parsley*
- *1 egg*   • *Barbecue sauce*

What To Do

Heat the oven to moderate - 180°C and grease a large loaf tin. Combine all the above ingredients in a mixing bowl except the milk and water and the barbecue sauce. When they are very well mixed add the milk and water and mix until smooth. Carefully spoon the mixture into the loaf tin and smooth down the top. Bake in the oven for 30 minutes. Remove and drain off any fat. (Parents will need to help with this part of the recipe). Invert the meat loaf onto a baking tray and cover with barbecue sauce. Bake for a further 45 minutes.

Delicious served with baked vegetables and greens. Makes enough for 6.

activity

53

HOME-MADE MUSIC

ABORIGINAL RHYTHM STICKS 4+

Australian Aborigines use rhythm sticks in their ceremonial dances and music. Make some simple rhythm sticks with the children so they can keep the beat to songs they know.

What You Need

- *Lengths of dowel or broom handles*
- *Ruler*   • *Saw*
- *Pencil*   • *Paints to decorate*

What To Do

Carefully measure the dowel or broom sticks into equal lengths and then saw off. You may need to sand the ends if they are a little rough.

Show the children some books with Aboriginal art so they can decorate their rhythm sticks authentically.

When they are dry, sing some songs that you all know with strong beats, and bang your rhythm sticks to the beat.

activity
54

BOTTLETOP TAMBOURINES 4+

Children love percussion-type instruments and many of them are very easy to make. Make these simple tambourines with the children and start a home-made band.

What You Need

- *Offcuts of pine*
- *Metal bottletops - beer bottle tops are ideal*
- *Nails* • *Hammer*

What To Do

The children will love helping you make these simple percussion instruments. Most timber yards or furniture manufacturers will let you have small offcuts of pine. Simply help the children hammer four to six bottle tops into each small piece of pine. Don't hammer the nails in all the way - leave some room for the bottle tops to shake around.

They can simply shake the wood in time to the music or bang it on their other hand to the beat.

Sing lots of songs you all know with strong beats - nursery rhymes are ideal or songs like 'Frere Jacques'.

activity
55

DIFFERENT DRUMS

4+

Make a variety of simple home-made drums for the children to play. Simple instruments will help develop your children's sense of rhythm.

What You Need

- *Containers - cardboard cylinders, tins, cardboard rolls from fabric shops*
- *A variety of 'skins' for the drums - plastic, thin rubber sheeting, greaseproof paper, wrapping paper and balloons*
- *Strong rubber bands* • *Cord*

What To Do

The children will love helping you make and decorate these simple drums

Simply cover a variety of cardboard cylinders and tins with different 'skins' using the strong rubber bands to hold the skins on the drums.

To make some of the skins even tighter for higher sounds, you can dip pap in water first and stretch it on wet.

Show the children how to play the drums by tapping the skin with their fingers.

You can attach cord to the sides of some of the drums so they can wear the round their necks and be a marching band.

(One of the advantages of these home-made drums is that they are not noi enough to have the neighbours up in arms!)

activity

56

JINGLE POLES

4+

Many bush bands use these simple poles and they are a great instrument to play and keep the beat with.

What You Need

- *Broom handle*
- *Beer bottle tops*
- *Nails*
- *Hammer*
- *Rubber doorstop*

What To Do

Begin by hammering holes in all the bottle tops first. Then hold the broom handle securely in a vice while you hammer the bottle tops down all sides of the broom handle. Hammer them in groups close enough for them to touch and rattle. Only hammer the nails into the bottle tops a little way so they can really rattle well.

Screw a rubber doorstop onto the end of the pole.

Put on some bush music and the children will love playing the jingle pole along by bouncing and banging it on the floor in time to the music.

activity
57

MUSICAL JARS

4+

A simple way to make music together.

 ✓
 ✓
 ✓
 ✓
 ✓

What You Need

- *4-6 similar empty glass bottles (coffee jars are ideal)*
- *Metal spoons*

What To Do

Leave one bottle empty, then fill the others with varying amounts of water, and fill one completely. Add a little food colouring to the water to make the water level easy to see.

Let your children experiment with the different sounds the bottles make by tapping them with the spoons. Arrange them in order so they can hear the notes go higher and lower.

After they have played for a while, ask them to close their eyes and listen carefully while you tap the bottles. Can they tell you which one is being tapped?

Later, they might like to tap (gently) other household items to hear the sounds they make.

activity

58

RICE MARACAS

4+

Children love making music. Make some simple rice maracas with them and they will love playing them and following the beat of their favourite songs.

What You Need

- *Paper cups* • *Felt pens*
- *Masking or insulating tape*
- *Uncooked rice*

What To Do

Fill a paper cup about half full of uncooked rice and then place an empty cup on the top. Your children can help hold them firmly and steadily in place while you join them together with tape. Now they can use their felt pens to decorate the maracas in bright colours.

Make a few with different amounts of rice in each one. For different sound effects you could use dried pasta, beans or split peas.

Shake out some different rhythms and see if they can copy them.

activity
59

SIMPLE GUITAR

4+

Help your children make a very simple guitar out of an old shoebox. It won't make the lovely sounds of a real guitar, but your children will enjoy strumming it just as much.

What You Need

- *Shoebox with a lid* • *Scissors*
- *6-8 rubber bands of different sizes (use thick ones that won't break easily)*

What To Do

Cut a hole in the lid of the shoebox about 8 cm in diameter. Put the lid back on the shoebox and press down hard on the lid so the rubber bands won't actually touch it and deaden the sound.

Now stretch the rubber bands right around the box and position over the sound hole.

As your children pluck the rubber bands they will hear the different sounds.

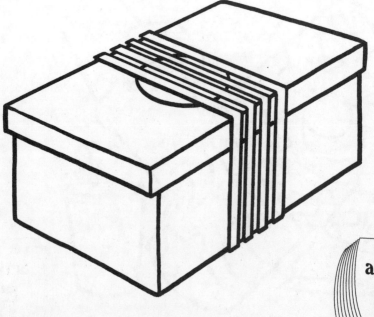

activity

60

COMB SYNTHESIZER

6+

Show your children how to make music with a comb and their lips!

What You Need

- *Comb*
- *Tissue paper*

What To Do

Tell your children you are going to make a music synthesizer that does not need electricity. Wrap a few layers of tissue paper around a comb and hold it up to your lips and hum. See if your children can recognise the tune. Now it's their turn. Ask them if it tickles their lips! Make one for yourself and make a comb band.

activity
61

SOFT DRINK BOTTLE MUSIC   6+

Pre-schools and kindergartens have long been the best recyclers of junk. Plastic soft drink bottles have many uses - for storage, pouring in the water trough, for scoops in the sand pit and even for musical instruments. Save some and make a wind ensemble with your children.

What You Need

- *Plastic soft drink bottles*
- *Water* • *Food colouring*

What To Do

Making music out of a plastic soft drink bottle is incredibly simple. Just hold it up to your lips and gently blow across the top of the empty bottle. You can vary the sounds by putting different amounts of coloured water into some of the bottles and making a whole range of sounds. Lots of cheap musical fun.

activity
62

HOME-MADE PIANO

8+

This is a great idea for older children to try, or an adult could make it for the younger children.

What You Need

- *Offcuts of pine*
- *Bolts, washers and wing nuts*
- *Drill*
- *Saw*
- *Vice*
- *Paddlepop Sticks*
- *Plastic flower pots*

What To Do

This idea is based on a thumb piano which originally came from Africa. Begin with two pieces of pine about 15 cm long and 4 cm wide. Drill through both pieces of wood at both ends and then bolt through the two pieces of wood with a long bolt.

Push the paddlepop sticks into the space between the pieces of wood. Begin with only a small piece of paddlepop stick poking out and work up to a long piece so the pieces resemble the short to long keys on a piano. The short sticks will make the high notes and the long sticks will make the low notes. Tighten up the wing nuts when all the paddle pop sticks are in place.

Put the piano on a hard, flat surface, hold it down firmly with one hand and you will be able to pick out simple tunes with the other hand. If you want more resonance, place the piano on two plastic flowerpots which have holes cut out of each side, and the notes will echo through the holes.

The children will love their simple home-made piano. Perhaps older children could use their local library to research the origins of this strange instrument.

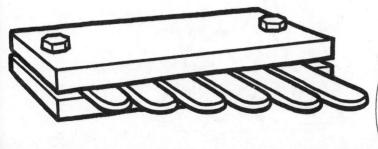

activity

63

INDOOR PLAY

BASH A BAG

2+ ✓

 ✓

Let your young children use up some energy and get rid of the 'Terrible Two's' aggression with this simple activity.

What You Need

• *A bag made of strong paper, plastic or fabric*
• *String* • *Newspaper* • *Wooden spoon*

 ✓

What To Do

Your two-year-olds will love helping you tear up the newspaper and roll it into balls to fill the punching bag. When it's full, tie it tightly with string and attach a string to hang it from a hook or doorway. (Make sure it will not hit anything precious.)

Your children will have a great time bashing away at the bag with a wooden spoon.

activity

64

BOX FUN

Lots of good fun, cheap creative play!

2+

What You Need

- *Cardboard fruit boxes of all sizes*
- *Other props such as cardboard cylinders, broom handles, sheets, rugs* • *Masking tape*

What To Do

On wet days when the children are driving you crazy, drive to your local fruit shop and they are usually happy to let you load up as many fruit boxes as you can fit in your car. Let the kids loose with the boxes and their imagination, and they will spend hours making tunnels, cubbies, towers and other creations.

When they have lost interest in building cubbies, save the boxes to make box cars or enlist their help to tidy up their toys and store some away in boxes for other rainy days.

activity

65

DETERGENT BOX BLOCKS

2+

Junk materials often make the best play toys for young children and, by recycling packaging, you are saving money and the environment.

What You Need

- *Square laundry detergent cartons*
- *Coloured or patterned contact*

What To Do

Many laundry detergents now come in block shaped cartons. They make ideal building blocks for your children. After wiping them out, tape the lid closed securely with masking tape and then cover with coloured or patterned Contact. (Contact can be bought by the metre from most hardware stores.)

Store the blocks neatly in the largest basket you can buy and add to the supply as you wash! My son uses his for building towers, making cities to go with his train set, making castles and other myriad uses.

Challenge your children to a competition to see who can build the highest tower before it falls down. If you have toddlers they will love it if your older children build towers for them to knock down!

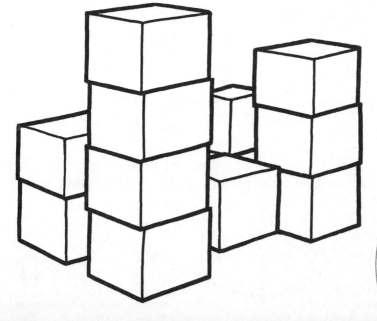

activity

66

DRESS-UPS

2+

Dressing up is an important part of young children's play. It is the way they practise for life. Provide a variety of dressing up clothes for them and they will play happily for hours acting out the family roles and relationships they see around them.

What You Need

- *Cardboard box*
- *Glue*
- *Variety of dressing up clothes and props*
- *Scissors*
- *Old magazines*

What To Do

Your children can help decorate a cardboard box to hold the dressing up things. They can cut out magazine pictures and 'collage' them all over the box until it is totally covered. While they are busy doing this, collect the clothes and props to put in it.

Talk to the family; older relatives may have hats, wigs and beads to donate. Sometimes a visit to an opportunity shop can yield wonderful dressing up clothes for little expense. When choosing accessories and clothes make sure they can be put on easily and worn safely. You may have to take up hems, thread elastic through waistbands to make them smaller, and perhaps even replace tiny buttons and fasteners with velcro. This way, their dressing up play need not always involve an adult.

The dressing up collection might include - necklaces, bangles, clip on earrings, shorts and T-shirts, coats, trousers, ties, belts, dresses and skirts (the frillier the better), lacy nighties and petticoats, pantihose, stockings or tights, shoes and boots, handbags, purses and wallets, scarves, shawls and glasses (without the lenses).

If you can sew you might like to sew some special dressing up clothes; look in the pattern books for dressing up clothes suitable for young children.

Birthday or Christmas gifts might include a special dressing up outfit such as a fairy costume, Bananas in Pyjamas, Batman or pirate gear.

activity

67

Extend your children's imagination with dress-up clothes.

KITCHEN PLAY

2+

As well as helping you in the kitchen with simple tasks, older toddlers love playing make-believe with some of your kitchen gadgets!

What You Need

- *Unbreakable bowls, spoons, ladles, baking trays, muffin tins, measuring spoons, plastic jugs and cups*
- *Playdough or water*
- *Large plastic sheet or plastic tablecloth*

What To Do

On a hot day your children will love 'cooking' outside with water - measuring, stirring, pouring and mixing. Add a few drops of food colour to the water and they will think it's great!

On cooler days, spread the plastic sheeting down, give the children some playdough and the kitchen items and they will 'cook' happily for ages. A cardboard carton turned on its side makes a great pretend stove. Draw some 'hotplates' on the top with a felt pen and put a biscuit rack inside for the oven shelves.

activity
68

SILLY WALKING

2+

This has been a favourite bedtime routine with our young child for some time.

What You Need

• *Time!*

What To Do

Bedtime routines vary in all families, but 'funny walking' is one we use that I thought I would share with you. If you bring routines into bedtime, it often makes putting young children down for the night easier.

When it's bedtime my child and I take it in turns to be the leader for 'silly walking'. As we go through the house playing 'follow the leader' he gets ready for bed - a small drink of water stop in the kitchen, a kiss for Dad in the lounge, toilet stop and then brushing teeth stop in the bathroom. Then he happily snuggles down for a bedtime story and kiss goodnight!

activity
69

SURPRISE BAGS

2+

There are many times when you will have to keep your young children amused and quiet, in an aeroplane or train, visiting someone in hospital, or perhaps just in a waiting room. Surprise bags are great for times like these.

 ✓

 ✓

What You Need

 ✓

• *Fabric bag* • *Interesting things to put inside it*

What To Do

Make or buy a fabric bag to hold the surprises. Collect things as you see them and have a bag ready to take with you when you need it in a hurry.

Some suggestions for things to put in the bag are:

• A new paperback book to read together
• Notebook or scribbling block
• Packet of coloured pipe cleaners
• Large wooden beads and plastic thread for threading
• Peggi-beads and board for building towers
• A new jigsaw puzzle stored in a plastic bag
• Threading cards
• Finger puppet
• Magnifying glass
• New small toy or car
• Unbreakable mirror

activity
70

WET DAY OBSTACLE COURSE 2+

Going through an obstacle course helps develop body co-ordination, control and balance.

 ✓

 ✓

What You Need

- *Furniture*
- *Pillows*
- *Towels*
- *Balloons*
- *Household Items*

 ✓

What To Do

On wet days when the kids are going 'stir crazy' why don't you set up an indoor obstacle course. (Make sure precious ornaments are safely out of the way first!).

Some ideas -

Crawling through the legs of the dining room chairs
Under a coffee table (watch those heads)
Tie a cord between two chairs to slide under on their tummies
Make a tunnel out of chairs, cushions and a rug
Play leap frog, stepping from towel to towel (only on carpet so they don't slip)
Tie some balloons under a table and crawl through without moving any
Roll up some towels and make a long 'balance beam'

For the older children (or when your children need new challenges) let them try the course balancing a bean bag on their heads, or do it holding a sock in each hand.

Time them to see who completed the course in the shortest time. Graph the results together.

Your children will enjoy altering the course but make sure you emphasize the safety aspect and check their alterations.

activity

71

ANIMAL SHADOWS

4+

Lots of fun and great for the developing imagination of your children.

What You Need

• *Lamp*
• *Hands*

What To Do

Shine a light on to a wall in your children's darkened room. Try and make as many different sorts of animal shadows on the wall with your hands as you can. Start with simple ones and see if you and your children can create some more, or try some of the ones listed below.

For children who are frightened of the shadows and who often think they 'see' strange things in a room at night, this game might make them less afraid of the dark.

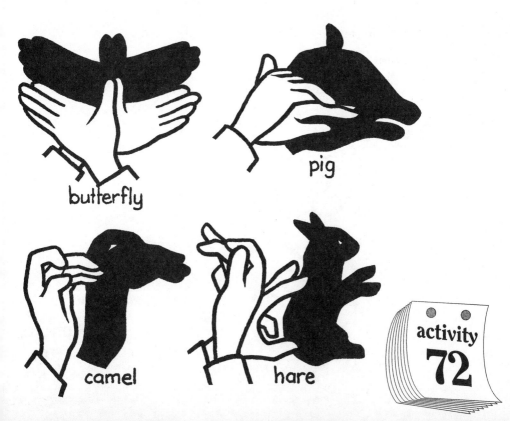

butterfly

pig

camel

hare

activity
72

BALLOON BOUNCING

4+

An activity to help your children learn their body parts and gain mastery of them.

 ✓

 ✓

What You Need

• *A blown-up balloon*

What To Do

 ✓

Encourage your children to toss the balloon in the air and stop it touching the floor. Count together and see how many times they can tap it before it comes down.

Encourage them to keep it up using other parts of their body - head, elbows, knees, feet, back etc.

Challenge your children further by seeing if they can -

Keep two balloons up at once.
Lie on the floor and keep the balloon up with their feet.
Hop on one foot and use their knee to bounce the balloon.
Jump around holding the balloon between their knees.

activity

73

CLOTHES PEG RACES

4+ ✓

A great finger motor pre-writing game to play with your children.

 ✓

 ✓

What You Need

- *Two players*
- *10 pegs each in two containers*
- *A clothes airer or clothes line strung between two chairs*

What To Do

Each player has a container with ten pegs. When you say 'go' they have to clip their pegs onto the line. They can only use one hand (the other hand stays behind their back).

If you have lots of children, you can divide them into two teams for this game and one player puts the pegs on and the next takes them off.

Lots of fun and a great activity to develop finger muscles ready for writing.

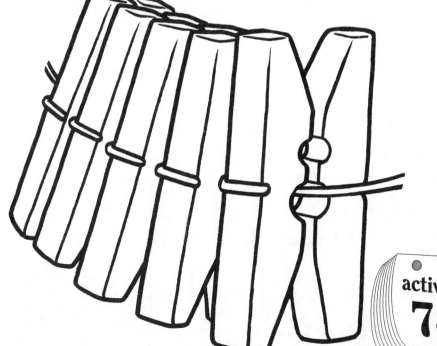

activity

74

CURTAIN PUPPET THEATRE 4+

Make a simple puppet theatre and your children will love putting on their own 'productions' with the home-made puppets they have been making.

What You Need

- *Calico or other cheap white fabric*
- *Hooks* • *Stretch wire*
- *Your sewing machine*
- *Acrylic or fabric paints*

What To Do

To calculate the width of the puppet theatre, measure the width of your children's bedroom doorway and double it. For the height, have your children kneel in the doorway. Measure just above their heads so they'll be hidden and add enough for a hem at the top and bottom.

Sew up the curtain and thread the stretch wire through the top and attach to a hook on either side of your children's bedroom doorway.

I am sure they will want to decorate the puppet theatre with acrylic paints or fabric paints but take it down again and do it outside.

When it's dry, hang it up and 'on with the show'. When not in use, roll it up and store it in the wardrobe.

activity

75

DRESSING FAST

4+

Give your children practice in dressing themselves with this game. It's fun to do on their own, but even more fun to do if they have a friend over to play.

What You Need

• *Dressing-up clothes -*
  Mum and Dad's old clothes work well for this game

What To Do

Give each child a pile of similar clothes - maybe a shirt, pair of long pants, socks and a hat each. Say "go" and they must run to their pile of clothes, put them on over their own clothes, and do up all the buttons and fasteners. Then they run back to you.

Don't forget to have a camera handy! This game is lots of fun at birthday parties, as well as being terrific practice for doing up buttons, clips and zips.

If you are playing it with your children on their own, they can try to beat the clock, or use an egg timer.

activity
76

FOOTPRINTS

4+

A fun way to help teach your children right and left.

 ✓

 ✓

What You Need

- *Cardboard* • *Pens* • *Scissors*

✓

✓

What To Do

Draw around your children's left foot and cut it out.
Use this shape as a template and make at least ten more.
Do the same with their right foot. Give them cutting practice by letting them help you cut out the shapes.

Blu-Tack the feet in a walking pattern around the house and your children have to follow them.

Sometimes it could be a treasure hunt with a surprise at the end!

Vary the difficulty by making the footprints further apart, or perhaps a hopping section.

activity
77

FUNNY FEET

4+

 ✓

Make some 'Funny Feet' with your children for them to wear and add to their dressing-up box. Watch the imaginative games begin.

 ✓

What You Need

 ✓

• *Egg cartons* • *Rubber gloves*
• *Strong cardboard* • *Pair of Dad's old socks*

 ✓

What To Do

 ✓

You can make a variety of 'Funny Feet' or just one pair.

Cut two egg cartons in half and use the top halves to make some claw feet. Cut the tops in half again and cut triangular shapes around the sides (see below) so they look like claws. Your children can attach them to their feet (or hands) with rubber bands. Hey presto! Instant tigers!

Wearing old rubber washing up gloves on the ends of their feet, they can be a platypus, seal or a duck.

Make clown or 'big' feet by wearing a pair of Dad's old socks with some strong cardboard inside.

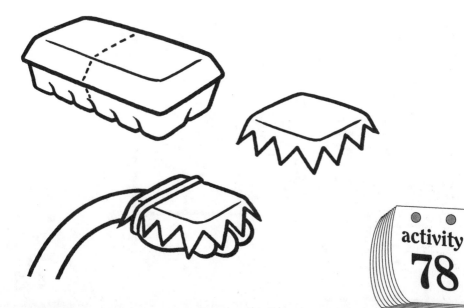

activity
78

NEWSPAPER WALK

4+

A good inside game to play with the whole family. (But don't play on the carpet or the newsprint may mark it)!

 ✓

 ✓

What You Need

• *2 or more players*
• *2 sheets of newspaper per player*

 ✓

What To Do

Mark out a starting and finishing line. Each player stands on the starting line with their two pieces of paper in front of them. When you say 'Go', the players must get to the finish line without touching the floor. To do this they must walk on one piece of paper and then put the other piece in front of them. They then pick up the first piece, place that down in front and then walk on that.

The first player to reach the finishing line by only walking on their newspaper sheets is the winner. The children love watching Mum and Dad have a go at this too, so go on, be a good sport and give them a laugh. Think how good all the bending is for the waistline!

activity
79

PLAYING SHOPS

4+

Solve the problem of wet day boredom by helping your children set up a 'pretend shop'.

What You Need

- *Large cardboard cartons or child size table*
- *Coins • Crayons • Paper • Scissors*
- *Items for the shop*
- *Props such as plastic bags, a toy cash register or a plastic shopping trolley*

What To Do

Help your children make a shop with cardboard cartons or a table. Raid the pantry together for tins and packets they can borrow for the shop.

To make money, Blu-Tack some coins to the table, place a piece of paper over them and show them how to rub over the coins with a crayon to get the coin rubbings. Help the children cut them out. If they have a toy cash register they can use that for the shop, otherwise help them find a container for the takings.

Make a shopping list and visit their shop - they'll love serving Mum!

activity
80

EASTER EGGS

6+

Eggs are traditionally associated with our Easter celebrations. Decorate some eggs with your children and serve coloured boiled eggs for breakfast on Easter Sunday.

What You Need

- *Eggs* • *Birthday cake candles*
- *Food dyes* • *Masking tape*

What To Do

Make up strong solutions of red, yellow and blue food dyes. (White eggs dye best so try and find a dozen at a supermarket with lots of white eggs).

Boil the eggs for at least ten minutes. Hard boiled eggs are best to use with younger children and will last as decorations for the Easter period out of the 'fridge, (unless you live in the tropics). However with older children you can use blown eggs which of course, while more fragile to work with, will last much longer.

To blow eggs use a large tapestry or darning needle and make holes at both ends - larger at one end than the other. Use the needle to carefully pierce the yolk sac a few times. Blow from the smaller hole end making sure you get all the egg out of the shell or later the egg will smell. Save the egg for scrambled eggs, omelette or other cooking. Blown eggs must be decorated before blowing.

To decorate, give your children a thin birthday cake candle to draw interesting designs on the egg. If you want to have multicoloured eggs, wrap sections of the egg with masking tape. Then use a spoon to dip the egg in the food dyes. Remove the masking tape gradually and you will end up with multi-coloured decorated eggs.

activity **81**

INDOOR HOCKEY

6+

Hockey is becoming a very popular sport in our schools. Show your children how to play this simple table-top variety - great for bored kids on wet days.

What You Need

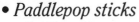

- *Table-top*
- *Books*
- *Paddlepop sticks*
- *Paper*
- *Masking tape*

What To Do

On a large table position thick books all around the edges to form the sides of the hockey field. Leave a space at each end to be the goal to shoot through. Each player has a paddlepop stick for a hockey stick. To make the ball, roll a piece of paper into a ball shape and wrap masking tape around it to secure it. Let the game begin.

The players stand at each end behind their opponent's goal and take it in turn to shoot the 'ball' towards their goal. Stay around because, like most family games, an umpire is often needed!

activity

82

MARBLE BOWLS

6+

Make a bowling alley for your children's marbles with them. A good game to play before bedtime or on wet days.

What You Need

- *A box - a shoebox is ideal, or a cereal box will do*
- *Scissors*
- *Paper*
- *Marker*
- *Marbles*

What To Do

Cut arches out of the bottom of the box for the marbles to roll into. Above each arch mark the score. Mark a spot on the floor for the players to roll from.

The competitors take it in turn to roll six marbles towards the box. If a marble goes through an arch, the player earns that number of points.

Appoint a score-keeper (parents are great at this) so there will be no arguments. The first player to reach a certain score - perhaps 50 or 100 - is the winner or, if it's before bedtime, the player with the highest score at bedtime!

activity
83

PING PONG BLOW

6+

This was a favourite game of my sister and I when we were younger. Like many families, we had a table-tennis table set up under the house and we both loved playing it. But we also loved this simple game of blowing the table tennis ball.

What You Need

- *A ping pong ball*
- *A large flat surface - a table is ideal*

What To Do

This game is almost incredibly simple and yet it will keep children occupied for hours. One child is at one end and another child at the opposite end. They take it in turns to blow the ball to the opposite end (or side of the table for younger players without so much puff!). If you can blow your ball past your opponent, you score a point. You cannot touch the ball with your hands - you must only blow to keep it from going over the end of the table.

Lots of simple fun and a great inside game on wet, boring days.

activity
84

COIN SPINNING

I am indebted to my mother-in-law for this activity. She and her brothers and sisters loved playing this when they were children.

What You Need

• *coins* • *pins*

What To Do

Carefully hold the coin between two pins, exactly opposite each other, and gently blow on the coin to make it spin. See who can make their coin spin the fastest. When they have mastered the trick see if they can do it with other coins.

Make sure that the pins are put away safely when this activity is over and keep them out of the reach of younger children.

activity
85

COLLECTIONS

Being a collector will help your children develop organisational skills and scrounging abilities.

What You Need

- *Try to encourage your children to collect more unusual items than football or basketball cards.*
- *Some things your child might like to collect:-*

Autographs	Shells	Rubbers
Badges	Keys	Drink coasters
Beads	Labels	Stamps
Book marks	Marbles	Stickers
Bottle tops	Match boxes	Matchbox cars
Crystals	Corals	Bus or train tickets
Buttons	Pencils	Dolls
Cards (greeting)	Postcards	Dolls clothes
Coins	Rocks	Tazos

What To Do

The most difficult part of any collection is finding the best way to store it. Photo albums are great for storing items like bus tickets, postcards, labels and cards. Badges can be pinned on bedroom curtains, and a cork notice board in your children's room can display lots of items also. Large clear bowls (fish bowls or tanks are ideal) can hold other collections.

Encourage your children to be selective collectors - keeping double-ups for swapping with their mates or other collectors.

If you have a computer at home and are linked into the Internet, this is a great way to meet up with other collectors for swaps.

activity
86

PLAITING

8+

Many children have never learnt to master this interesting skill. Learning to plait will help develop your children's manual dexterity.

 ✓

 ✓

What You Need

• *Lengths of heavy wool, thin rope or twine or long strands of interesting fabric.*

 ✓

What To Do

Tie together three equal lengths of the plaiting material. It's a good idea when your children are learning to use three different colours to make it easier for them. Attach the plaiting material to the back of a chair or a door knob and separate the strands so there is a left, a centre and a right strand.

The left hand strand goes over the centre one and then the right hand strand goes over the new centre one, the original left strand and so on. Continue plaiting, left to the centre, right to the centre. Tie off when the plait is finished.

If your children are really 'into' this activity they could plait lots of lengths of fabrics (great way to empty the rag box) and later you can help them sew them together to make an old-fashioned rag mat to put beside their bed or use as a bath mat.

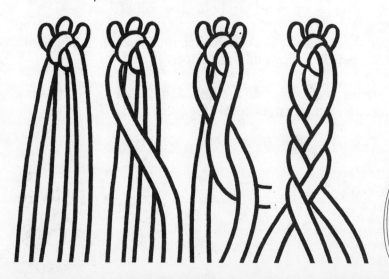

activity

87

SECRET MESSAGES

8+

Children love intrigue and mystery and writing secret messages to their best friend (so brothers and sisters can't read them) will become a favourite activity.

What You Need

- *Paper* • *Birthday cake candles*
- *Watercolour paint*
- *Lemon juice* • *Cotton buds*

What To Do

There are two ways to write secret messages. The simplest way is to write on a piece of white paper with a candle. When your children's friends want to read the message, they paint over the paper with a wash of water colour paint.

The other method is to write the message with lemon juice using a cotton bud. When it's dry, dip the paper in water and the message can be read.

activity
88

LANGUAGE AND LITERACY

BAA BAA BLACK SHEEP 2+

Teaching young children lots of nursery rhymes helps improve their language and memory, and develops important rhythmic patterns.

What You Need

• *Time together*

What To Do

If you cannot remember the words of Baa Baa Black Sheep, they go like this:

>Baa baa black sheep
>Have you any wool?
>Yes sir, yes sir, three bags full.
>One for the master and one for the dame
>And one for the little boy
>who lives down the lane.

Teach them the next verse too:

>Moo moo Jersey cow
>Have you any milk?
>Yes sir, yes sir, three buckets full.
>One for the master and one for the cat
>And one for the little boy who wants to get fat.

Talk about wool together, how it is shorn off the sheep and what happens next. Find a woollen garment or blanket for your children to feel.

activity
89

HUMPTY DUMPTY

2+

Teach your young children lots of nursery rhymes. This will help develop not only their language but also their memory and sense of rhythm.

 ✓

 ✓

What You Need

• *Eggs, etc.*

What To Do

If you cannot remember it, Humpty Dumpty goes like this:
 Humpty Dumpty sat on a wall
 Humpty Dumpty had a great fall
 All the King's horses and all the King's men
 Couldn't put Humpty together again.
There are some other funny ends you can use.
Two of my favourites are:-
 Humpty Dumpty sat on a wall
 Humpty Dumpty had a great fall
 All the King's horses and all the King's men
 Had bacon and eggs for breakfast again.
Or:
 Humpty Dumpty sat on a wall
 Humpty Dumpty had a great fall
 All the King's horses and all the King's men
 Said 'Oh, not scrambled eggs for dinner again'.

After your children have learnt the rhyme, why not make scrambled eggs together for dinner. They will love beating the eggs, adding the milk and buttering the toast. My family loves grated cheese in our scrambled eggs, so your children can help grate the cheese too. Later, carefully wash up the egg shells, roll them with a rolling pin to break them into small pieces and help your children make an egg shell collage picture of Humpty Dumpty.

Or have boiled eggs for tea, then carefully wash the empty shells out and fill them with cotton wool. Help your children to pour enough water onto the cotton wool to make it damp. Place the egg in an egg cup and together draw on Humpty's face with felt pens. Sprinkle the top with bird or grass seed, water regularly, and in time Humpty will grow a magnificent head of hair.

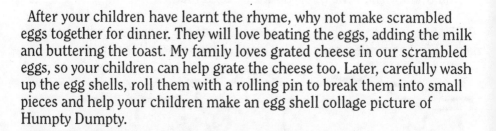

activity
90

'I HAD A LITTLE NUT TREE'   2+

When you teach your young children nursery rhymes, you are building their foundations of literacy.

What You Need

• *Time together*

What To Do

If you cannot remember the rhyme, it goes like this.
If you can remember the tune, sing it to your children too.

I had a little nut tree
Nothing would it bear
But a silver nutmeg and a golden pear
The King of Spain's daughter came to visit mm
'Twas all for the sake of my little nut tree.

Macadamia nut trees are very easy to grow and are not only a most attractive small tree, but a useful culinary addition to your garden. If you live in a colder climate go to your local plant nursery and find out what sort of nut tree you could grow - chestnuts are wonderful trees to plant too. Make this your children's special tree and their responsibility to help water and care for it.

By the time the tree is big enough to bear, they will be old enough to help crack the nuts with a hammer or nutcracker or the vice in Dad's workshop.

activity
91

JACK AND JILL

2+

When you teach your children Nursery Rhymes you help develop not only their language, but also their memory and sense of rhythm.

What You Need

• *Time together*

What To Do

If you cannot remember the Nursery Rhyme, it goes like this:

JACK AND JILL WENT UP THE HILL
TO FETCH A PAIL OF WATER,
JACK FELL DOWN AND BROKE HIS CROWN
AND JILL CAME TUMBLING AFTER.

UP JACK GOT AND SAID TO JILL,
AS IN HIS ARMS HE CAUGHT HER,
YOU'RE NOT HURT, BRUSH OFF THE DIRT,
AND NOW WE'LL FETCH THE WATER.

On a hot day, fill a large bucket with water in the garden. Your children will love pretending it is the well and filling lots of smaller buckets and containers from it. Give them some small stones, too, and they can improve their throwing skills by throwing them in the 'Wishing Well'.

DON'T FORGET TO ALWAYS SUPERVISE WATER ACTIVITIES WELL!!

activity
92

LITTLE MISS MUFFET

2+

 ✓
 ✓
 ✓

  ✓

When you teach your young children Nursery Rhymes you are helping to develop their language, memory and sense of rhythm.

What You Need

• *Time together*

What To Do

If you cannot remember the Nursery Rhyme, it goes like this:

LITTLE MISS MUFFET SAT ON A TUFFET
EATING HER CURDS AND WHEY,
THERE CAME A BIG SPIDER WHO SAT DOWN BESIDE HER
AND FRIGHTENED MISS MUFFET AWAY.

Today's name for Curds and Whey is junket. See 'Junket' in the book and make some together with your children.

Go for a walk in the garden together early in the morning and see if you can find some spiders' webs. They look beautiful sparkling in the early morning light with dew from the night on them. Keep watching them for a few days and see what the spider is going to have for his dinner!

activity
93

READ READ READ

2+

Young children love books and, as teachers, we know that children who have had lots of stories and books read to them at home are more likely to become good readers. They know what books are for and they want to learn to read for themselves.

What You Need

• *Time with your children* • *Books*

What To Do

Make a special time each day to read to your children. My time with our four year old is before rest time in the afternoon and before bedtime at night, but any time is fine. It's nice to snuggle up together and enjoy some good stories. If you don't already belong, join your local council library. Going to the library was a tradition my parents started with me and I have continued with my child. He loves choosing books - last week he took out eleven and he would love me to read them all every day!

Books make great gifts and, as children get older, Gift Vouchers to bookshops make great presents as they can choose books that they specially want to read. Make reading together a part of every day with your children - no matter how old they are!

activity

94

COPY THE PATTERN

4+

Copying and recognising a pattern is an early reading skill. Children who have difficulty naming and matching colours often have difficulty learning to read. Provide lots of activities like this for your four and five year olds and read to them lots and you will make learning to read easier for them.

 ✓
 ✓
 ✓
 ✓
 ✓

What You Need

- *Large wooden beads*
  (available from Bead or Craft Shops)
- *Plastic threading string or long shoe laces*
  (available from Craft Shops)   • *Felt pens*
- *White cardboard*   • *Clear Contact*

What To Do

Work out some simple patterns with the beads - two long yellow beads, one round red bead, two long yellow beads and so on. Or perhaps three square blue beads, two long green beads and one small round brown bead, and then repeat. Copy the patterns onto pieces of the cardboard and then contact to make them last longer.

See if your children can copy the bead pattern cards by threading the beads onto the strings. Make sure your children understand to copy the pattern from left to right - the same progression as reading. Can your children name all the bead colours and tell you what shapes the beads are? Can they continue the pattern?

Later, see if your children have gained an understanding of patterning by seeing if they can create their own patterns. Perhaps they could make some for you to copy.

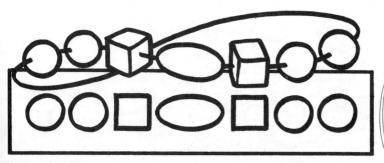

activity
95

DROP THE PENNY

A listening game to play with your children.

What You Need

- *Large glass jar*
- *Small items made from different materials to drop into the jar, for example: coins, comb, dice, pencil, plastic clothes peg, safety pin, marble, sinker*

What To Do

Show your children the small objects and let them listen while you drop them, one by one, into the bottle.

Then put a blindfold on them and drop the items in again, one by one, to see if they can tell you what has been dropped.

This activity is harder than it sounds - have a turn yourself and see how good your listening skills are.

activity
96

FAVOURITE STORY TAPES   4+

If your children have a favourite story that they want to read time and time again, turn it into a fun activity together and suggest you record the story on a tape so they can listen to it themselves.

What You Need

- *Cassette player that young children can use*
- *Blank cassette tape* • *Story book*

What To Do

Suggest to your children that they might like to have their own special recording of their favourite story. Find a bell to use to indicate when it is time to turn the page. If there are any sound effects that could be added, experiment with these. Your children will love adding the sound effects. They could also ring the bell when it is time to turn the page.

When the taping is completed, play it back, and you will have a big laugh hearing the results.

Perhaps you could also tape some Nursery Rhymes or Fairy Tales for your children to listen to.

Nothing replaces reading books with your children and having a nice cuddle together, but good listening skills are essential for school and this activity will help develop your children's listening skills in a fun way.

activity
97

GO-TOGETHERS

4+

An activity to help develop your children's thinking and language skills.

What You Need
- *Objects that go together:*
  cup and saucer
  pencil and rubber
  pen and lid
  knife and fork
  toothbrush and toothpaste
  hair brush and comb
  needle and cotton
  key and lock
  hammer and nail
  shoe and sock

What To Do

Explain the object of the game to your children then put half the objects on a tray for your children to see.   Place the other half of the 'go-togethers' in a pillowcase.

Your children have to reach in, feel an object, guess what it is and then say what it goes with.

'It feels like a sock and it goes with the shoe.'

activity
98

HICKORY DICKORY DOCK 4+

When you teach your young children nursery rhymes, you are developing their language and listening skills as well as improving their memory and sense of rhythm.

What You Need

- *Time together*
- *Cardboard*
- *Marking pen*
- *Scissors*
- *Split pins*

What To Do

If you cannot remember Hickory Dickory Dock, it goes like this:

Hickory Dickory Dock
The mouse ran up the clock
The clock struck one
The mouse ran down
Hickory Dickory Dock
Tick! Tock!

Make a simple clock face and large and small hands out of the cardboard. Attach them with the split pin. Mark the hours on the clock and begin to show your children important times during the day - this is when we have breakfast, this is when Daddy leaves for work, this is when we go to Playgroup and so on.

They won't learn to tell the time until they're older, but activities like this will help their understanding of how time passes.

activity
99

"I SPY"

4+

A good observation game that can be adapted for various age groups.

What You Need

• *At least 2 players*

What To Do

You can play this game anywhere with your children as it is a great boredom alleviator. Think of something you can see around you (if you are playing it in the car, it obviously can't be something that flashed past 5 kms back!).

Say 'I spy with my little eye something beginning with '??' (whatever letter)'.

For non spellers use a colour or a shape:
'I spy with my little eye something that's red or something that's round'.

For beginner readers, it may help to use the letter pronunciation, eg. something beginning with 'dee' (the letter D).

If you children can't guess the answer, give them clues.

With older children, increase the difficulty by using lots of words:
'A T S I T C'
(e.g. ' Anna's Teddy sitting in the chair').

An oldie,
but a goldie!!

activity

100

NURSERY RHYME RHYTHMS

4+

Listening to rhythms in rhymes and songs is a great activity for your children.

What You Need

- *Time*

What To Do

Clap out a nursery rhyme your children know well. If they cannot identify it after a few turns, give them some clues, for example: 'It's about two children going up a hill' or 'It's about a little girl who was frightened by something'.

When they guess correctly, they can clap one out for you to guess. A great game to play in the car on long family trips.

activity
101

ALPHABET SPOTTING

6+

 ✓
 ✓
 ✓
 ✓

 ✓

A good game to play together when you are driving in the car or just a thinking game to play at home.

What You Need

- *Clipboard with paper*
- *Pen or pencil*

What To Do

Before you start out on a long drive, help your children write the alphabet down the side of the paper.

As you drive along, first look for something beginning with A, write it down, then B, then C and so on. Your children can be the scribes but help them with any difficult spelling. If you want to make a competition out of it, your children can write beside each word who spotted the item.

If you are playing it at home, make it more difficult by thinking of categories, eg. animals, foods, clothing etc. that begin with different letters of the alphabet.

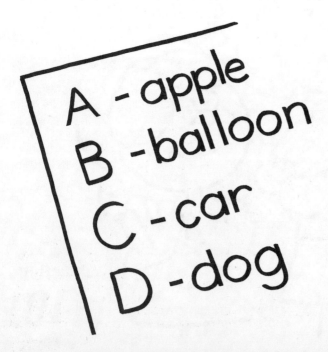

activity
102

ANIMAL, VEGETABLE OR MINERAL 6+

A good guessing game to play with older children.

What You Need

• *Players*

What To Do

Think of an object or person 'IT'. The categories in this game are Animal (people, animals, insects, etc.), Vegetable (plants) and Mineral (iron, innate objects).

Your children can then ask twenty questions to try and determine what 'IT' is. Except for the first question which traditionally asks if it is 'Animal, Mineral or Vegetable' all the other questions are just answered with a 'Yes' or a 'No'.

The person being asked the questions keeps track of the number of questions asked. If there is more than one person asking the questions, the first person to guess the answer on or before the twentieth question has the next turn.

Hint: If you find your children are getting 'bogged down' by the questions give them some clues until they begin to understand the game!

activity
103

DIARIES

6+

A good way to start a lifetime habit of writing.

What You Need

- *Spiral notebook with blank page on one side and lines on the other*
- *Drawing and writing materials*

What To Do

Keeping a diary is a great way for your children to record their activities, thoughts and feelings. Starting young they can build an excellent writing habit for later life.

Writing in a diary each day may be too ambitious for younger children so perhaps an entry a week may be more realistic. Encourage them to draw a picture of something that happened that week and then write the events of the week on the page opposite. Younger non-writers can tell you what to write for them. Make sure each entry is dated at the top of the page. Remind other members of the family that diaries are private and only looked at with the owner's permission.

activity
104

'I CAN'

6+

Make an "I Can" book with your children to boost their self esteem and their writing skills.

What You Need

- *Paper* • *Stapler*
- *Drawing and writing materials*

What To Do

To encourage your children's increasing independence, talk together about things they can do now on their own. These might include dressing themselves, tying their shoelaces, keeping their rooms tidy, riding their bikes without training wheels, playing a sport, swimming or using a knife and fork correctly. I am sure you and your children will be able to do lots more.

Staple together pieces of paper to make a book. On the front they draw a picture of themself and write their name. (Don't forget to date the book so in years to come they can enjoy reading it again).

On each page they draw a picture of themselves doing something they can do on their own. Underneath the picture they write ?. "I can ?????..". You will have to help them with some of the words.

Read it together, share it with the rest of the family and their teachers, who may like to try it with the rest of the class too. Then put it away in their special box to keep for the future.

activity
105

JOB CHART

Begin a family job chart with your children to encourage them to help more and for all the family to share tasks.

What You Need

- *Large sheet of cardboard*
- *Pens for drawing* • *Paper*

What To Do

Together talk with your children about all the chores the family needs to do to keep your home running smoothly. List them together, e.g. ironing clothes, washing, vacuuming, dusting, cleaning the bathrooms, washing floors, shopping, putting shopping away, putting out the garbage, collecting the mail or papers, cooking, setting the table, mowing the lawn, gardening, hosing the garden, sweeping paths, cleaning the car, making beds, tidying up. I am sure you can think of lots more - it makes me exhausted just thinking of them all!

Your children then draw a small picture of each chore.

Rule the cardboard so there is a space for each family member and room for the chores. Your children can place the chore pictures beside the family member who does them. (At this stage in most families Mum will probably be doing a lot more than the rest!). If this is the case, talk to your children and the other family members about sharing more of the load.

A happy family works together.

activity
106

LETTER BINGO

6+

A fun game to teach letters to your children.

What You Need

- *Cardboard*
- *Pens*
- *Scissors*

What To Do

Cut the cardboard into bingo cards and divide each card into nine squares. Randomly, write alphabet letters on the bingo cards (use upper and lower case letters so your children learn both - for example 'Aa').

Cut up lots of small squares of cardboard and write the alphabet letters on them, making sure you have all the letters you have used on the bingo cards.

Give each child or family member a board and place the letter cards in a pillow case. Pull them out one at a time and hold them up for the players to see, as well as calling them out. This will help younger players. When a player has that letter on their board, they cover it with a token - buttons or small coins are ideal. The first player to cover their board calls out 'Bingo'.

For older children make it more difficult by calling out words, and they have to place a token on the first letter of the word.

Another version is that the winner also has to think of a sentence made up of words that begin with the letters on the bingo board in sequence,

e.g.

Tt	Hh	Cc
Ii	Ll	Uu
Dd	Oo	Bb

The sentences are usually very funny. The example above might be: "The hairy cat is lying under Dad's old bomb".

See if they can make the sentences as unusual as possible.

activity
107

MY BOOK ABOUT MY BIRTHDAY 6+

This activity provides a chance for your children to see the value of print. Making their own books will develop your children's vocabulary and counting skills.

What You Need

- *Notebook or scrapbook*
- *Writing pen*
- *Felt pens, coloured pencils or crayons.*

What To Do

Like most parents we still talk about the joy and wonder of the day our son was born. Share this with your children and make a personalised book with them describing what happened that day.

Buy a scrap book and note book and help your children write the story or write it for younger ones. Your children can illustrate it or perhaps even use some of the photos taken that day (or have photocopies made very cheaply at your nearest photocopying shop).

This book is something your children will treasure especially in the years to come when they become parents. Together you have helped create a family heirloom.

activity
108

RHYMING CHARADES

6+

Listening to rhymes is an important pre-reading and reading skill. Make sure that from an early age you read your children lots of rhyming nursery rhymes, poems and books and encourage them to 'spot the rhyming words'.

What You Need

- *Paper* • *Pen*

What To Do

Together with your children think of rhyming word families, e.g.

Dog, log, frog, bog
Cat, mat ,fat, pat, rat
Pen, men, ten, when

With younger non-readers just think of the rhyming words together.

Then say 'I'm thinking of a word that rhymes with Bill' and act out the rhyming word, e.g. taking a 'pill'.

See if your children can not only guess the correct answer, but write it down for spelling practice.

When they guess correctly it's their turn.

activity
109

DICTIONARY CODE

8+

Using their dictionary will seem like fun as your children unravel this fun code.

What You Need

• *a dictionary* • *paper and pencil*

What To Do

When your children are not around, use their dictionary. Begin by printing a simple message onto a piece of paper and then change the message into code. To do this you'll have to look up each word in the dictionary and then replace it with the word that immediately precedes it. For example 'What do you want for dinner tonight?' becomes (in my dictionary) 'Wharfinger djibba Yorkshire wanion fop dinky tonicity?'

Your children must use the same dictionary you have used or they will never be able to uncode the message. When they are proficient at this code they can make up some messages for you to uncode. They will love teaching their friends this easy code - see if their teacher can work it out too.

This activity is not only fun but will really increase your children's skill with their dictionary.

activity

110

DIRECTORY ASSISTANCE 8+

Give your child practice at using a telephone directory.

What You Need

- *A cassette recorder and a blank cassette*
- *Telephone directories - white and yellow*

What To Do

Ask your children to pretend they are the telephone operator and, on a blank cassette, record five 'requests' for directory assistance. Use real names from both the white and yellow pages for these.

Leave enough blank tape between each request for your child 'operator' to give their name and then respond to the request. This is not only great practice at using the telephone directories but also will help them become more familiar with using a cassette player.

When they are competent at the task, record some more for them to find, or perhaps they will enjoy looking up the names and addresses of businesses they know or friends at school.

activity
111

FAMILY TREE

8+

Help your children learn more about your family and understand family relationships by making a simple family tree together.

What You Need

- *Memories (talk to Grandma and Grandpa)*
- *Old family photos*

What To Do

Get a large sheet of cardboard and print in the names of your family with your children. Add dates of births, deaths and marriages. Go back through as many generations as you know about. Research together the ones you don't know by asking grandparents and older relatives.

If possible add photos to your family tree. Look for family resemblances and compare clothes and hair styles of today with those of your ancestors.

Encourage your children's awakening interest in the past by looking for historical books from the library or by visiting an historical museum together. Encourage your children to talk to their grandparents and great-grandparents about the 'olden days' so those memories are not lost.

Perhaps all of this might inspire you to organise a family reunion!

activity
112

FIND THE WORD GAME

8+

A game that tests the word skills of all the family!

What You Need

- *Pencils and papers*

What To Do

Find a long word and give all the players a pencil and paper. The players must try to make as many words as possible from the letters in the long word. The player who makes the most words is the winner.

A few rules - all the words must contain at least three letters; a letter may only be used more than once in a word if it is contained in the main word more than once; and it's a good idea to set a time limit for the game - perhaps ten minutes.

So, from the word CATASTROPHE you could make words such as:

TASTE, TROT, STAR, STRAP, TASTER, TOAST, PERT, TOTE, PEST, HAT and lots more!

activity
113

HANGMAN'S NOOSE

8+

A spelling game for older children - a great fun way to test your older children's weekly spelling list from school.

What You Need

• *Pencil* • *Paper* • *2 players*

What To Do

Select a word your children know and draw a line for each letter in the word at the bottom of the piece of paper. Your children try to guess which letters are in the word. If they are correct, write the letter on the line. If they are wrong, add a line to the hangman's noose drawing. If you draw the whole hangman they have lost!

hangman

activity
114

JUMBLED WORDS

8+

Help improve your children's spelling skills in a fun way.

What You Need

- *Weekly spelling list from school*
- *Pen* • *Paper*

What To Do

Most schools send home a weekly spelling list for children to learn. Ask your children for the list and jumble up the letters of each word. Write them down with a line beside each for the correct spelling. Your children will have lots of fun figuring them out.

Time them each week to see if they are getting faster at working out the solutions.

PLIGSELN	SPELLING
UFN	FUN
IHWT	WITH
UBEJMLD	JUMBLED
ODWRS	WORDS

activity
115

LETTER STEPS

8+

Help your children improve their spelling and word skills with this word-making activity.

What You Need

• *Paper* • *Pencils*

What To Do

Do a few of these word-making activities together first, then give your children some to try on their own.

Choose any two words that have the same number of letters, such as MINE and SAND. The object of the game is to change only one letter at a time   until the first word is changed into the second. However, you must make a new word at each letter change. So, for MIND and SAND it might go like this:

MINE / MANE / SANE / SAND

or SOAP to PEAR like this:

SOAP / SOAR / SEAR / PEAR

Other words may take longer than three steps to change
- try KITE to FAZE

KITE / MITE / MATE / MAZE / FAZE

The person who can change one word to another with the least number of changes wins that round and chooses the words for the next go. Sometimes it simply cannot be done and that round is declared a draw.

activity
116

LOOK AT WORDS

8+

Making up anagrams (a mixed up word using the same letters) is lots of fun and a great way to improve your children's spelling ability.

What You Need

• *Paper* • *Pencils or pens* • *Dictionary*

What To Do

Think of some words from which to make anagrams - beginning with one of your children's names perhaps. Our son's name is ANDREW, which can become WARDEN. If the names are short, your children could make anagrams with their middle name or surname.

The weekly spelling list from school is a good place to start, and encourage your children to use the dictionary to check their spelling, incorporating practice in a fun game.

Making up anagrams will help your children look at words in a new way.

Have a family competition to see how many words you can all make. Timing your children with the clock or the stove timer works well also.

Have them take their spelling list of anagrams to show their teacher, who might get the whole class involved.

---

andrew — warden
dust — stud
stage — gates
mate — tame

activity
117

SHOPPING LISTS

8+

Encourage your children's writing skills by helping them make the shopping list before you go shopping together.

What You Need

• *Paper* • *Pen or pencil*

What To Do

Before you do your weekly grocery order, sit down with your children and together write the shopping list. Your children can do the writing - if they do not know how to spell a word, they might be able to look at packets in the pantry or advertising brochures - or just encourage them to have a go. Help them make the list in an organised fashion, with fruit and vegetables together, dry staples together, and so on.

Take the list when you do the shopping together and they can use it.

Shopping may take a little longer but you are helping your children learn an important life skill.

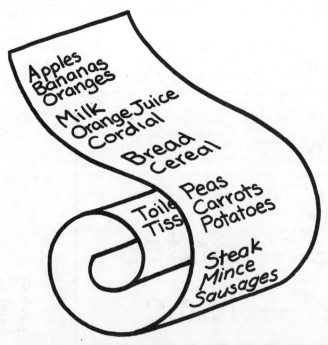

activity
118

SPELLING WORD BINGO

8+

Hearing children's spelling can be a fairly laborious task for parents night after night, and yet it is an essential one if we want our children to become competent readers and writers. Turn the Spelling Homework into fun by making some Spelling Word Bingo cards with the weekly Spelling List.

What You Need

- *Spelling Homework List from School*
- *Cardboard* • *Marking pens*

What To Do

Rule up a few boards divided into room for ten words. Choose words from the latest spelling list, as well as ones they have had to learn previously for revision. Make matching word cards with some more cardboard. Dad may like to play also.

Call out the words and the players put a coin or button, or other marker, on the correct word. The first player to match all the words is the winner and receives a small treat. Now take away the boards, call out the words and see how well they have been learnt.

Playing Spelling Bingo will help your kids learn their spelling in a really fun way.

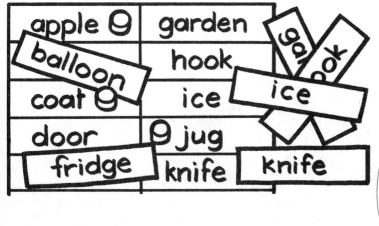

activity

119

SPELLING WORD CROSSWORDS 8+

Make the weekly spelling homework more interesting by making up some crossword puzzles for your children to do.

What You Need

- *Paper* (*If you need help, buy a crossword book*
- *Pens* *from your newsagent and this will give you*
- *Time* *some ideas for setting out.)*

What To Do

Draw up a simple crossword and think of the clues. Don't use cryptic clues for younger children. As your kids get better at crosswords, you can increase the difficulty of the clues.

Give the crossword to your children to work out. When they have finished, see if they have learnt the spellings in a fun way. If they still need help, practise them together.

DOWN
1. It bounces
2. Boys name

ACROSS
1. It floats.
3. It's green.

activity
120

TALKING TO GRANDMA

8+

Most children share a special bond with their grandparents. Encourage this and their interest in history by making a book about when Grandma or Grandpa was their age.

What You Need

- *Paper* • *Stapler* • *Glue*
- *Pens for drawing and writing*

What To Do

Next time you visit the grandparents suggest to them that they talk to your children about when they were their age.

They could talk about their favourite toys and activities, things they did together as a family, games they played with their brothers and sisters, their family, their home, differences between life then and life today. Your children will be fascinated.

Encourage them to write down what they learn. Their grandparents may have some photos they can have (or have copies made) to add to their book.

Keep it as a special family heirloom.

activity
121

ANIMAL FAMILIES

10+

Helps older children learn both dictionary skills and animal group names.

What You Need

- *Dictionary*
- *Paper*

What To Do

Do your older children know the names of animal family groups? We all know a group of birds is a flock or fish a school, but what about some of the more unusual ones.

Write down the following words on a piece of paper.

Brace
Clouder
Drive
Flock
Gaggle
Herd
Kennel
Knot
Pace
Rather
Swarm

Your children can use their dictionary to find which animal group it describes. They can then illustrate the group.

activity
122

PENPALS

10+

A way to encourage your children to write letters and also to learn about new places through a new friend.

What You Need

• *Cousins who live far away, a friend from interstate met on a holiday, or friends who have moved away, can all be penpals. Ask your school's headmaster if you can't think of anyone - schools often have sister schools in other states or countries. Or help your children write to a school in a state or country stating their name, age and that they are interested in finding a penpal. If you have a computer, look on the Internet!*

What To Do

When your children start writing their letters, keep a photocopy of each one and keep the originals of the ones they receive in a large photo album. They will be fascinating to read in years to come.

Encourage your children to send lots of photos of themselves and family photographs to their penpal also. Hopefully, they will return the favour - photos of themselves, their family, home, school and environment.

Happy writing!

activity
123

LET'S CREATE

BOX CARS

2+

Making cheap play props like this together helps develop your children's imagination.

What You Need

- *Cardboard box*
- *Felt pens*
- *Paper plates, pieces of cardboard, foil pie plates*
- *Acrylic paint*

What To Do

Make a box car for your children. Cut the flaps off the top and bottom of a cardboard box except for the flap at the front. Your children can paint the box at this stage - maybe racy red, or British racing green! When it's done, stick paper plates on the side for wheels and foil pie dishes on the front for headlights. Straps go over your children's shoulders to hold it up and they're off and racing.

Boxes could also be aeroplanes or boats! Just use your imagination and, of course, your children's.

activity
124

BREAKFAST CEREAL THREADINGS 2+

Breakfast cereals can make pretty necklaces and bangles and keep the children amused while they make them. Threading is also an excellent eye-hand co-ordination activity.

What You Need

- *Bodkin or a large tapestry needle*
- *Wool* • *Breakfast cereal loops*

What To Do

Help your children thread their needles or bodkins and tie a cereal loop at the end of the wool to secure it. If you don't want your younger children using needles, wrap some sticky tape around the end of the wool to make a firm threading and they thread with that.

Older children will enjoy making colourful patterns as they thread. Younger ones will enjoy eating their creations at the end!

activity

125

BUSY BOX

2+

Children are natural 'recyclers' and our junk is often their treasure. Make a 'Busy Box' together and start collecting~

What You Need

• *strong cardboard box with a lid (apple boxes are ideal)*
• *glue* • *paper*

What To Do

Help your children decorate their 'Busy Box.' You could use some of their paintings or drawings, magazine pictures, wrapping paper or magazine illustrations to collage all over the box. Alternatively, they could paint it with bright acrylic paints or, after covering it with white butcher's paper, they could decorate it with crayons or felt pens.

Find a suitable place to store the Busy Box that's easily accessible for everyone - perhaps in a wardrobe or in the bottom of your linen cupboard.

In the busy box we keep a shoe box that contains the 'tools of trade' - good quality children's scissors (children will easily become frustrated with learning to cut if scissors aren't sharp), sticky tape in a good quality dispenser, masking tape, glue bottle or glue pen and a stapler. A pencil case could hold crayons, felt pens, and coloured pencils. Now you're ready to start collecting!

activity
126

BUSY BOX COLLECTION 2+

 ✓
 ✓
 ✓

Here are some suggestions for junk, art, and collage materials you may like to collect and store in the Busy Box. Some smaller materials will be best stored in individual containers (margarine, butter, or take-away containers make ideal small storage containers).

What You Need

 ✓

• *aluminium foil, beads, bottle tops, bark, cardboard, cylinders (lunch wraps and toilet rolls), cellophane, chalk, chocolate wrappers, confetti, corks, cotton reels, cotton wool, cotton wool balls, dried flowers, egg cartons, egg shells, fabric scalps, feathers, grasses, gumnuts, gift wrappings, glitter, iceblock sticks, leather scraps, leaves, lolly wrappers, paint sample sheets, paper, paper bags, paper clips, patty cake papers, pebbles, pine cones, pipe cleaners, ribbons, rulers, sandpaper, seeds, sequins, scraps of lace, sawdust, straws, styrofoam, stickers, sponges, string, toothpicks, toothbrushes (old for painting), wallpaper samples or off-cuts, wool and yarn, anything else you can think of.*

What To Do

I've started with this activity because having a collection of art materials and junk on hand is a necessity for many of the activities in this book. Children are natural recyclers and our junk is often their treasure. Make a Busy Box together and start collecting.

activity
127

COLOURFUL BLOB PAINTINGS 2+

Children love surprises and blob paintings really appeal to their sense of surprise.

What You Need

- *Paper* • *Brushes*
- *Colourful paints (acrylic paint works well, or make up a strong paint with wallpaper paste and food dyes).*

What To Do

Help the children fold their papers in two. Next show them how to put blobs of paint on one side of the paper. Fold the paper over and press it down hard. When they open up the paper-wow! What is it? When the blob painting is dry they can draw around their picture and cut it out.

Maybe it's a butterfly or a monster! Anything is possible with children's imaginations.

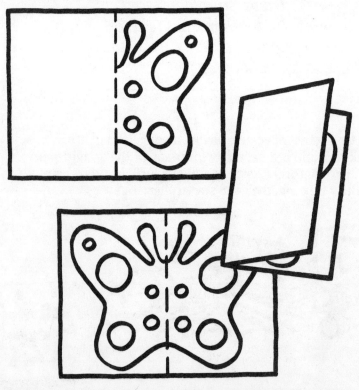

activity

128

COLOURFUL PLAYDOUGH

2+

 ✓
 ✓

 ✓
 ✓

Make up a batch of simple cooked playdough for your children. It will keep them occupied for ages and provide a great outlet for their creativity.

What You Need

- *1 cup plain flour* • *1/2 cup cooking salt*
- *1 cup water* • *1 tablespoon cream of tartar*
- *1 tablespoon cooking oil*
- *Food colouring or powder paints*

What To Do

Your children will enjoy helping you make the playdough. With a wooden spoon, mix the flour, water, salt and cream of tartar in a saucepan over a medium heat until thick. When it has cooled, add the oil and knead well on a floured board.

Divide it into at least six balls and add a different colour to each ball until you have blue, red, yellow, green, purple and orange playdough (or any other colours you would like).

Put each colour into a separate container and encourage your children to create playdough pictures or dioramas. When they have finished, help them sort out the colours to put back in their containers for another day, rather than mixing them all together. Happy modelling!

activity
129

CREATIVE PLAYDOUGH

2+

 ✓

 ✓

Playing with playdough gives children the opportunity to be creative while it helps develop their finger muscles, so important for writing at school.

What You Need

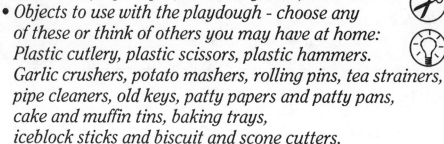

• *A batch of playdough (see activity **131**.)*
• *Objects to use with the playdough - choose any of these or think of others you may have at home: Plastic cutlery, plastic scissors, plastic hammers. Garlic crushers, potato mashers, rolling pins, tea strainers, pipe cleaners, old keys, patty papers and patty pans, cake and muffin tins, baking trays, iceblock sticks and biscuit and scone cutters.*

What To Do

Make up a batch of playdough with your children and give them all or a selection of the items mentioned above. They will play happily for ages. Make sure you are close by to admire their creations and to try making some of your own.

activity
130

EDIBLE PLAYDOUGH

2+

Make a simple edible playdough that younger children will enjoy playing with.

What You Need

- *Peanut paste*
- *Milk powder*
- *Sugar*
- *Edible food colouring*

What To Do

Younger children often want to eat 'regular' playdough. If this is happening with your younger children, put away the regular playdough until they are older and can understand not to eat it, and make them a batch of edible playdough.

Simply mix one part of peanut paste to one part of milk powder and half a part of sugar. Double or triple the quantities depending on how much you want. Add some food colouring if desired.

activity
131

FINGER PAINTING

2+

Finger painting provides a wonderful sensory activity for young children. They love the squishy, slimy feeling as they draw with the finger paint.

What You Need

- *1 cup of cold water*
- *2.5 litres of boiling water*
- *1 cup of soap flakes*
- *1 cup of laundry starch*
- *1/2 cup of talcum powder*
- *Powder paints or food colouring*

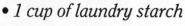

What To Do

Begin by dissolving the starch in cold water. Add the boiling water slowly while stirring. Add the soap flakes and talcum powder and, last of all, the paint or food colouring. Allow to cool.

Carry a low table outside or spread a plastic sheet or tarp on the grass for the children to paint on. Make sure they are wearing a painting smock or an old shirt of Dad's over their clothes!

When they draw a special picture in the finger paint you can make a print of it by pressing a piece of paper on it.

Finger painting prints make great wrapping paper, too, so store some away for future birthday parties!

If you are game, feet painting is lots of fun, too! Make sure there is a bucket of soapy, warm water handy for cleaning up.

activity
132

FIRST LACING CARDS

2+

A new skill to teach your young children.
A good pre-sewing activity and great for eye-hand
co-ordination.
(See Hole Punch Pictures for older children-168)

 ✓

 ✓

What You Need

- *Thick cardboard* • *Lacing materials*
- *A hole punch*

✓

✓

What To Do

Visit your local picture framer for a supply of the thick card they use for picture mounts. Cut the card into simple shapes or even shapes like toys or perhaps fruit. (You are only limited by your imagination and your art ability!!).

Now punch holes around the edge of the shapes at least 3 cm apart for your children to lace through.

With younger children it is safer not to use a bodkin so you will need threading materials that are stiff enough to thread without one. Old shoe laces are ideal, plastic lacing is cheap to buy by the metre from craft shops or most haberdasheries. You can even dip the ends of wool or string into melted candle wax or a strong laundry starch solution to stiffen them. Make sure you tie the lacing through a hole to start. When your children are a little older they will enjoy making their own Hole Punch Pictures. (See activity **168**).

activity
133

PAINT PALETTE

2+

A cheap and easy way to provide paints for your children.

 ✓

 ✓

What You Need

 ✓

- *A plastic egg carton or an ice cube tray*
- *Powder paints (available at toy shops)* • *Fine brushes*

 ✓

What To Do

 ✓

Water colour palettes can be quite expensive to buy but you can easily make your own at home.

Put some powder paint into the segments of the egg carton or ice cube tray and then add a little water to mix. (Hint: make the colours quite strong). Allow to dry and harden for a few days.

Give your children some paper, small brushes or cotton buds and a jar of clean water to wash the brushes and they'll have lots of fun painting with their own home-made palette.

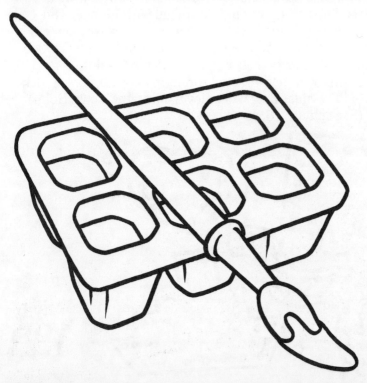

activity
134

PHOTO PUZZLES

2+

Make some simple cheap puzzles for your young children to put together.

What You Need

- *Large photos of your children, family or home*
- *Clear contact (or have the photos laminated)*
- *Scissors or a Stanley knife*
- *Strong cardboard • Craft glue*

What To Do

Use some large photos if you already have any or have some enlarged cheaply at your local photocopying shop. Your children will love doing a puzzle of their face, their whole body, one of the family, or perhaps their bedroom. Just use your imagination, or ask them!

Use craft glue to paste the photos onto the cardboard. When it is dry, contact over both sides or take it to have it laminated. Then use scissors or a Stanley knife to cut it into large puzzle pieces. As your children gain mastery of the puzzles, you can cut them into smaller pieces to increase the challenge.

Take photos of some of your friends' children and make them individual puzzles too - great cheap gifts, and everyone will be amazed at your creativity!

activity
135

SELF PORTRAITS

2+

Encourage your children to draw lots by always having lots of drawing paper, crayons, coloured pencils and felt pens available.

What You Need

• *time together* • *drawing materials* • *paper*

What To Do

Ask your children to draw a picture of themselves or a self-portrait. From an early age children should be encouraged to draw. Let them look in a mirror for inspiration or talk about the things they like doing best and they can draw themselves doing this. Another idea is to look at photos of them together and they can get ideas from these. Date and name these self-portraits and save them in a special place. You will be surprised when you look back together at how much their drawing changes each year.

activity
136

SOCK SNAKE

2+

Next time you find an odd sock, help your young children make it into a 'Sock Snake'. They will use it in their imaginative play and it will become a favourite friend.

What You Need

- *Old long sock*
- *Scrap paper to tear*
- *Coloured paper or stickers for the face*
- *Strong glue*

What To Do

Give your children a newspaper or other scrap paper to tear into small pieces for the filling. This is an excellent fine-motor activity to help strengthen their finger muscles.

When they have torn up enough, they fill their "snake", pushing the paper right down to the toe.

They might like to use stickers to make a face on their snake or cut out pieces of paper. Stripes or spots of paper add interest also.

Together, think of a funny name for the snake - maybe "Socks" or "Snakey"!

activity
137

TEXTURED PLAYDOUGH

2+

Add interesting materials to a batch of playdough to introduce your young children to new textures.

What You Need

- *A batch of playdough (see recipe on activity **131**)*
- *Sand • Rice • Confetti • Split peas*
- *Lentils • Dried beans • Glitter or small leaves*

What To Do

Make up a batch of playdough with the children and they will love helping you knead it when it has cooled a little. Then add one of the above texture materials to half the batch and another texture material to the other half. Try this with lots of textures and find out what the children enjoyed playing with the most.

activity
138

BALLOON HEADS

4+

Make a whole family of colourful 'Balloon Heads' for your children's dramatic play. Simple, cheap and lots of fun.

What You Need

- *Balloons* • *Plain flour* • *Water* • *Funnel*
- *Teaspoon* • *Permanent marking pens*

What To Do

Together, blow up the balloons and then deflate them. Put the funnel into the balloon's mouth and carefully spoon in as much flour as you can. Add a little water to make the flour pliable and tie up the balloon.

Your children will love making faces on their balloon heads and moulding them to make funny facial features - big ears, squashed noses and fat cheeks!

activity
139

BUBBLE PICTURES

4+

Help your children make beautiful bubble pictures. These colourful paintings make great wrapping paper for birthday presents, too!

What You Need

- *Margarine containers*
- *Washing-up detergent*
- *Powder paints*
- *Paper* • *Drinking straws*

What To Do

Half fill each container with water and add some powder paint and a little detergent. Place a drinking straw in each container. Show your children how to blow into the container until it is almost overflowing with bubbles. Press the paper on top of the container and when you take it off there will be beautiful bubble prints on it.

An alternative method is to place the straw in the bubble mixture and hold a finger over the end to retain some mixture, then your children blow lots of bubbles over the paper. As the bubbles burst they make colourful bubble prints on the paper.

Make sure that your children understand not to suck the liquid however!

activity
140

COLOUR MIXING

4+

Great fun and your children learn how colours are formed.

What You Need

- *Lots of glass jars or clear plastic containers*
- *Plastic eyedroppers (cheap to buy or save the ones that come with children's medicine)*
- *Red, yellow and blue powder paint*

What To Do

Help your younger children to half fill the containers with water (provide a jug for pouring the water, perhaps a new skill to learn). Older children will be able to manage it on their own.

Next help your children add some of the red, yellow and blue paint to three of the containers. They then add drops of colour to the jars with the plain water to make lots of new colours.

Arrange the finished containers on a shelf or table with the sun shining through them making rainbows.

Later they might like to add a mixture of cornflour and water to the jars and see the changes that occur -
- how the colours change
- the intensity of the shades
- how the clear colours become opaque.

Also see Eyedropper Painting - (activity **166**)
and Rose Coloured Glasses - (activity **156**)

activity
141

EGG SHELL PICTURES 4+

Help your children make an interesting textured picture from egg shells. They could also use them to decorate unique cards for birthdays and other special occasions.

What You Need

- *Dyed egg shells* • *Cardboard*
- *Strong glue* • *Plastic containers for storage*

What To Do

Save all the egg shells from cooking or from boiled eggs. Wash them well and dry in the sun before storing. When you have quite a lot you can dye them in batches, using strong solutions of food dye. Again, dry them well in the sun after dyeing. Your children will enjoy helping you with the dyeing, but don't forget to wear rubber or plastic gloves or your hands will look like the Incredible Hulk's!

Your children can then crush the egg shells with a roller or with a meat mallet. It is easiest to do this on a kitchen board covered with a tea towel. When they have finished, pick up the tea towel and pour the pieces carefully into a container for each colour.

Now they are ready to be creative with all the lovely dyed egg shells.

activity
142

FINGER PUPPETS

4+

Make some simple finger puppets with your children, then settle down with a 'cuppa' to watch the show.

 ✓

 ✓

What You Need

 ✓

- *Old gloves (washing up gloves are fine)*
- *Permanent felt pens*
- *Strong glue*
- *Wool, sequins, small buttons, other decorations*
- *Shoe box*

 ✓

 ✓

 ✓

What To Do

Cut off the fingers of a pair of gloves and help your children decorate them to make some finger puppets. Use the felt pens to draw faces or glue on small buttons or sequins for facial features. Make beards with cotton wool, dresses with scraps of fabric and hair with wool. You'll all have lots of fun thinking of details.

If your children want a puppet theatre for their puppets to perform in, this is easily made from a cereal carton or a shoe box. Stand it on end and then cut a window near the top for the puppets to perform in. Your children will enjoy decorating the puppet theatre too.

Gather the rest of the family, make some popcorn and sit back to enjoy the show.

activity
143

FLYING HELICOPTERS

4+

Make this fun flying object together. Launch it from the verandah and see how far it can fly.

What You Need

- *Scissors* • *Paper clip*
- *An old postcard or a small piece of cardboard*

What To Do

Measure and cut together a strip off the postcard 3 cm wide. In this strip, make two slits 2/3 of the length of the card as shown.

Hold a corner in each hand and twist and then bring them together and secure with a paper clip.

The kids will love dropping the helicopter from up high and watch it as it whirls around.

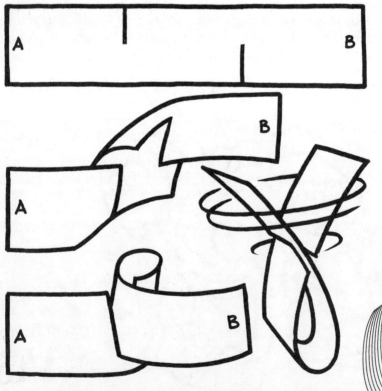

activity
144

HAND GLOVE PUPPETS

4+

Make some simple fabric puppets for your children to decorate.

What You Need

- *White cotton fabric (calico is ideal)*
- *Fabric glue* • *Felt pens*
- *Collage items such as sequins, buttons, wool, fabric scraps for decoration*

What To Do

Place your children's hand down on a doubled over piece of fabric approximately 20 cm x 15 cm.   Draw around the outline of their hand with a felt pen, leaving room for a seam allowance.

Stitch the puppet on your sewing machine and turn inside out and press flat with your iron.

Your children will have lots of fun decorating their puppet.   (Why not make quite a few - they can make enough for a puppet show!)   They might make the characters out of a fairy tale, perhaps Goldilocks and the Three Bears, or even their own family.   Settle down in front of their puppet theatre for a great show (see Puppet Theatres - activity **75**.)

activity
145

JUNK THREADING

4+

A great eye-hand co-ordination activity. Older children will also enjoy making their own jewellery.

 ✓

 ✓

What You Need

 ✓

- *Bodkins for younger children*
  - tapestry needles for older ones
- *Selection of different coloured wools*
  or embroidery cottons
- *Fine hat elastic for bracelets*
- *shapes cut from coloured cardboard or greeting cards*
- *Wide variety of threading materials such as:*
  milk bottle tops (punch holes in plastic ones with
  a hole punch)
  soft drink or beer bottle tops
  (use a hammer and nail to punch the holes)
- *matchboxes*
- *macaroni*
- *pieces of lace or other lovely woven fabrics*
- *cut up egg cartons (with holes punched in them)*
- *cardboard cylinder (cut into short lengths)*
- *straws*
- *dough or clay beads (baked in a slow oven)*
- *cotton wool balls*
- *patty cake papers*
- *paper beads (roll brightly coloured paper strips*
  around a pencil, glue and leave to dry)
- *buttons or old beads*

What To Do

Thread the bodkin or tapestry needle and knot near the top. Thread an object on to the wool and knot at the bottom. Your children then thread.

Keep all the threading items in take-away food or margarine containers for easy packing away.

activity 146

MAGIC PLAYDOUGH

4+

A fun way to help your young children learn how to make new colours.

What You Need

- *Basic recipe for cooked playdough (see Colourful Playdough - activity **129**.)*
- *Food colouring or powder paint*

What To Do

Make up the cooked playdough recipe with your children. When you have finished, divide it into six balls. In the middle of each ball of playdough hide some food colouring or powder paint (two balls each of red, yellow and blue).

First, give your children a ball with yellow paint hidden in it and one with red. As they play, the colours will appear and then combine to form orange. Magic!

Later, they can combine red and blue to make purple and blue and yellow to make green. All the balls combined will form brown playdough.

Talk with them about what they have learnt and about the new colours they have made.

activity
147

MAKE A MOBILE

4+

Young children love watching mobiles swing in the breeze. Help your children make one for their room or as a special gift for a new baby.

What You Need

- *Wire coat-hanger or ice cream container lid*
- *Bodkin • Wool or embroidery cotton*
- *Junk for threading (see Junk Threading - activity 146)*

What To Do

After your children have threaded four or five lengths of threading, tie them securely to a wire coat hanger or through holes punched in an ice cream lid. Make sure it is balanced, then hang on a hook in the ceiling of your children's room.

Mobiles are also great to hang above a baby's change table.

activity

148

MAKE A PLACE MAT

4+

Your picky eaters may enjoy meals more when they eat off their custom made place mat.

 ✓

What You Need

 ✓

- *A piece of thick cardboard cut to the desired size*
- *Clear contact*
- *Crayons, felt pens, collage materials*

 ✓

What To Do

 ✓

Leave decorating the place mat entirely up to your children. They could decorate it with collage materials, magazine pictures, draw or paint on it or even use dried leaves or flowers from the garden.

Fringing the edges can add a nice touch as well as provide useful cutting practice for younger children.

When the decorating is finished, cover completely with contact (top and bottom to protect against spills) or have it laminated. (Many photocopying shops or even your children's school or kindy have laminators and will do it for a small fee).

Perhaps your budding artists might like to make a complete set for the whole family and be responsible for setting the table too!

activity

149

MAKE A SOCK PUPPET

4+

Children love making puppets for imaginative play.

What You Need

- *Old socks*
- *Buttons*
- *Bits and pieces from your sewing box*
- *Permanent felt pens*
- *Needle and cotton*
- *Craft glue*

What To Do

If your home is like mine, whenever I clean out the drawers (particularly my husband's), there are always quite a few odd socks. It is one of life's little mysteries as to their mates - does my washing machine gobble them, or perhaps the dog? Anyway, your children will think it's great fun making them into puppets.

Younger children will need your help with the craft glue to glue on buttons for eyes and other bits or pieces, or mark a mouth with a felt pen.

Older children will enjoy the challenge of sewing on buttons and other decorations from your sewing box.

Sock puppets are limited only by your children's imagination, but one of the creatures I have found they most enjoy making out of socks is dinosaurs. Take your children to see the dinosaur exhibits at your local museum or read books about dinosaurs together, and their ideas will just flow.

It is also a great opportunity to teach your older children how to sew on their own buttons!

activity
150

MARBLE PAINTINGS

4+

Make some colourful wrapping paper with marbles for paintings

What You Need

- *marbles* • *paper* • *teaspoons*
- *containers of different coloured paint*
- *shirt or cereal boxes or a large plastic box*

What To Do

Put the paper in a large box. Put a few marbles into each different colour paint and use a teaspoon to lift out one marble at a time and put it in the box on top of the paper. Now show your children how to lift the box to roll the paint covered marble all around the box until all the paint has come off the marble and made marble tracks all over the paper. Your children repeat this until the paper is covered with bright tracks of colour. Keep the marble paintings for unusual wrapping paper for gifts.

activity
151

PAPER BAG PUPPETS

4+

 ✓

 ✓

 ✓

 ✓

Help your children make a whole collection of these and then put on a puppet show together for the rest of the family.

What You Need

- *Paper bags* • *Glue*
- *Scissors* • *Felt pens*
- *Scrap paper or other collage materials*

What To Do

Today, most supermarket bags are made of plastic, but some stores are becoming environmentally conscious and are again using large brown paper bags. These make fantastic puppets. Otherwise, buy a pack of brown paper lunch bags.

Your children can make their puppets any way they like, but perhaps they might like to cut or tear long strips of coloured paper for hair, add a cellophane mouth and draw large eyes. Don't forget that the bottom of the puppet is where the hand goes in!

Older children like making funny faces cut from different photos in magazines.

When it is finished, your children put their hand in and make the puppet talk!

Fat puppets are fun to make too. Stuff the paper bag with newspaper, insert a lunch wrap roll and staple or sticky tape the bottom. Hold the puppet by the cylinder and make it move.

Don't forget to take a photo of your children's great puppets and the puppet show for your family album.

activity
152

PERFUMED PLAYDOUGH

4+

Playdough gives children the opportunity to be creative and to explore a new medium.

What You Need

- *A batch of playdough*
  *(see activity **131** for the simple recipe)*
- *Essences such as strawberry, lemon, peppermint, vanilla or chocolate (look for these in the baking section of your supermarket)*

What To Do

Make up a batch of playdough and colour it to match the essence you are going to add - yellow for lemon essence, pink for strawberry and so on. Add plenty of essence so the smell stays in the playdough.

Make sure your children understand that this is a smelling experience and not a tasting one!

activity
153

PET ROCKS

4+ ✓

 ✓

 •

An oldie but a goldie!

 ✓

What You Need

- *Smooth creek or river bed rocks*
- *Paints or collage materials for decorations*

 ✓

What To Do

 ✓

We often have picnics near creeks or river banks covered with lovely smooth rocks.   Help your children select a rock to bring home for a 'pet'.   Younger children will be especially enchanted with this idea.

At home your children can characterize their pet rock with a painted face, or use collage materials glued on - perhaps some wool for hair, a button for his nose, a ric-rac braid mouth and so on.

It makes a great paper weight and the easiest pet to look after I know.

activity
154

PRINTING PLAYDOUGH

4+

 ✓
 ✓

Playdough is a simple, cheap medium that provides children with the opportunity to create and explore new materials.

What You Need

- *Batch of playdough (see Colourful Playdough - activity **129**.)*
- *Materials for printing, such as old keys, leaves, flowers, gumnuts, nuts and bolts, parts of the body such as toes, fingers and elbows, toy parts of Duplo, Lego or Brushblocks, stones, and kitchen items.*

 ✓
 ✓

What To Do

Show your children how to make interesting patterns and prints in their playdough with a selection of the materials suggested above.

activity
155

ROSE COLOURED GLASSES   4+

Children are fascinated by how looking through new colours changes their world.

What You Need

- *Cardboard toilet rolls or lunch wrap cylinders*
- *Scraps of different coloured cellophane*
- *Sticky tape or glue*

What To Do

Help your children use different coloured scraps of cellophane to cover one end of some cardboard cylinders to make coloured telescopes. Look through them to see your familiar world in a different way.

You can also cut the middle out of paper plates and replace it with cellophane to make a good 'view finder' or even take the lens out of old sunglasses or reading glasses to make 'coloured ones'.

See Stained Glass Windows - activity **176** for more colour ideas with cellophane.

activity
156

SAND PAINTINGS

4+

Children love the texture of sand and they will enjoy the novelty of painting with coloured sand.

What You Need

• *fine beach sand* • *powder paints*
• *large salt shakers (the sort you take on picnics are fine for this activity) or plastic containers without lids*
• *glue* • *paper or card*

What To Do

Put some fine sand into each of the plastic containers or large salt shakers and mix a little of the powder paint with the sand so you have a few colours of sand.

Next the children use the glue to "draw" a picture. If younger children find this difffcult, have them draw with a pencil first and then glue over their drawing. Now they sprinkle or shake the coloured sand over their glue picture. When they have dried, display them proudly.

Hint

Make some large numerals and alphabet letters on paper with the sand. Children enjoy tracing around these textured numbers and letters with their fingers and will learn them easily.

activity
157

SPLATTER PAINTINGS

4+

A quick and easy way to decorate paper.

What You Need

- *Containers of acrylic paint*
- *A brush per container*
- *Newsprint paper*

What To Do

Spread out the paper on the grass outside or peg some paper on an easel if you have one.

Show your children how to dip the brush in the paint and flick the brush with their fingers so the paint flies onto the paper.

Make sure your children wear a painting smock or an old shirt of Dad's over their clothes because this activity is fairly messy.

The splatter paper makes great gift wrapping paper or is also good for covering school books.

activity
158

SPRAY PAINTINGS

4+

Save all your old household spray bottles for this fun, painting activity.

What You Need

• *food colouring* • *water*
• *spray bottles* • *paper* • *pegs*

What To Do

This is definitely an outside activity and only to be done on a very still day! Mix up some food colouring and water in the spray bottles (make sure they have been very well washed out first).

Peg up some paper outside - if your children have an easel use that, otherwise peg the paper between two trees or on the fence. Show them how to spray with short, fine bursts and encourage them to use lots of different colours to see how the colours mix and new colours are made. Discourage them from spraying too much on each piece of paper - if the paper becomes too wet it will fall to bits. Keep the spray paintings for sensational, bright, wrapping paper.

Hint

If you don't have a painting smock to cover your children's clothes, put them in an old shirt of Dad's, done up back-to-front. On hot days let them spray paint in their togs - but don't forget the sunscreen.

activity
159

STOCKING BABY

4+

With a little help your children can make their own 'stocking baby' to love and cuddle.

What You Need

- *Pantihose* • *Elastic bands*
- *Scissors* • *Needle and cotton*
- *Filling - this could be cushion filling, cotton wool or old fabrics*
- *Buttons* • *Wool*

What To Do

Cut off the lower part of the pantihose below the knees and keep. Stuff and then knot the ends to form the baby's 'feet'. Use the lower legs to make the arms and, after filling them, sew the openings.

Take the rest of the pantihose and fill with the stuffing. Sew or knot the waistband to make the top of the baby's head. Twist a rubber band below its head to make its neck and, lastly, sew the arms onto the body.

Your children can help you make the baby's face. Buttons look great or perhaps embroider or felt pen on a mouth. Wool can be sewn on for its hair.

Your children might like to dress their baby in some of their own tiny baby clothes.

activity
160

TWINKLE TWINKLE

4+

Take your young children outside at night to look at the stars and teach them the old song Twinkle Twinkle Little Star. Next day, try this 'star painting'.

What You Need

- *White paint* • *Black paper*
- *Cardboard for stencils*

What To Do

Carefully cut out some cardboard stencils for your children to paint inside. Help them position the stencil on the black paper and paint the inside of the stencil with the white paint. Do this with lots of star shapes until they have their own beautiful starry nightscape to hang in their bedroom with Blu-Tack.

activity
161

ART IN THE DARK

6+

A good family activity to play at night, especially in storms when there is a power failure!

What You Need

• *Pencils* • *Paper*

What To Do

Hand everyone a pencil and paper and make sure they can draw comfortably. Turn out all the lights.

First, they write their name at the top of the paper, then tell them what to draw - perhaps a cow, or your house or Mum, or anything else you can think of. When everyone is finished, turn the lights back on and have a laugh at the results.

Move over, Picasso!

activity
162

BAKED BEADS

6+

Help your children make colourful necklaces for themselves or original gifts for others with this simple recipe.

What You Need

- *4 cups of plain flour*
- *1 cup of salt*
- *1 1/2 cups of cold water*

- *Acrylic paints*
- *Brushes*
- *Fishing line*

What To Do

Mix together the flour and salt and then add the water. Knead for at least ten minutes on a floured board (let your children help with the measuring and kneading). Measuring is a great maths activity and kneading is good for small muscle development. Knead until the craft dough is pliable and will not fall to bits.

Help your children mould it into interesting bead shapes. Use a nail, skewer or kebab stick to make a hole through the centre of each bead.

Bake the beads in a slow oven for 2-3 hours until they are hard and completely dry.

They look great painted in bright colours. Thread with fishing line when the paint is totally dry.

activity
163

BATIK FOR KIDS

6+

Conventional batik needs hot wax and this is dangerous with young children. Use this safe batik to make interesting fabric designs.

What You Need

- *Old detergent container*
- *Cold water dyes (available from chemists and supermarkets)*
- *White cotton fabric (sheeting material is fine) or T-shirts*
- *Flour*
- *Water*
- *Brushes*

What To Do

Together, make up a paste from flour and water and pour it into an old detergent bottle. Your children can squeeze the paste onto the T-shirt or fabric in whatever design they like. When the paste is dry, make up the cold water dyes, provide the brushes and they can paint the glue-free areas.

When the garment or fabric is dry they will have their own fabric art work. You could make the fabric into some great big comfy cushions on which to read books in their bedroom.

activity
164

DINOSAUR PUPPETS

6+

Kids are absolutely fascinated by dinosaurs. Research them together and help your children make a Dinosaur Puppet Stage and Dinosaur Puppets.

What You Need

- *Stiff cardboard*
- *Felt pens*
- *Glue*
- *Scissors*

What To Do

Fold a large piece of cardboard at both ends so it can stand on its own (see the diagram below). Your children can use their imagination to decorate it with dinosaur 'scenery' - rocks, mountains, perhaps a volcano, water, etc. Look in books about dinosaurs together for ideas.

They then draw or trace pictures of dinosaurs onto more cardboard and carefully cut them out. Tape stiff cardboard tabs about 10 cms long and 3 cms wide onto the dinosaurs to hold them. Cut slits in the puppet theatre where your children want the dinosaurs to move.

Place the puppet theatre on the edge of a table. Your children stand or sit behind the theatre and move the dinosaur puppets as they tell the story.

Help them work out a little play to perform for the rest of the family or for their class at school.

activity
165

EYE DROPPER PAINTING

6+

Teaches your children how to mix the three basic colours to form new ones.

What You Need

- *Plastic eye droppers (cheap to buy or save the ones that come with children's medicines)*
- *Red, yellow or blue powder paint or food colouring mixed with water*

What To Do

A good activity to do on a table or tarp outside or, if it's going to be an inside activity, spread lots of newspapers on your table.

Provide three jars or paint pots with the basic colours, red, yellow and blue and three eye droppers. Provide plenty of paper and let your children experiment with making new colours.

Encourage them not to make the paper too wet with paint or it tears when hung up. Wet paintings can be hung on a clothes drier to dry or even on the clothes line.

Sometimes it is fun to wet the paper first with plain water and see what happens when the colours are squirted on. (Use small bottles of food colouring.)

(Also see Colour Mixing - activity **141** for more eye dropper fun).

activity
166

FINGERPRINT CRITTERS   6+

Your children can use their imaginations to create interesting 'critters' from their fingerprints.

What You Need

• *Stamp pad or coloured felt pens*
• *Pens or coloured pencils* • *Paper*

What To Do

Show your children how to make fingerprints by pressing their index finger in the stamp pad, rolling it from side to side and then carefully place it on the paper and again roll it from side to side to produce a clear print.

If you don't have a stamp pad, they can colour their index finger with a non-permanent felt pen and then make a print.   (Have a cloth nearby to wipe fingers on - you don't want fingerprints all over the walls).

Then they add details to turn their fingerprints into whatever they like, such as birds, flowers, people, bugs, monsters or anything else they can think of.   Think of some of your own too!

activity
167

HOLE PUNCH PICTURES

6+

A new skill to teach your children that helps develop their fine motor skills.

What You Need

- *Polystyrene trays (butchers and greengrocers often use these) or thin card*
- *Felt-pens*
- *Hole puncher*
- *Threading materials*

What To Do

After your children have drawn a colourful picture on the card or polystyrene, show them how to punch holes around either the outline of the picture or the border. The holes should be about 3 cm apart.

Your children will then enjoy lacing in and out of the holes. Use a bodkin (blunt ended large needle) threaded with wool or thin embroidery cotton. If you don't want them to use a needle they could lace with plastic lacing (available by the metre from craft shops and haberdasheries) old shoelaces or wool or string that has a strengthened end made by dipping it into melted candle wax or a strong solution of laundry starch and allowed to dry.

The pictures can be hung up with another length of the threading material.

activity
168

JUMPING JACKS

6+

Make some Jumping Jacks with the children and give Dad a big surprise.

What You Need

• *Strong paper - typing or photocopy paper is ideal*
• *A strong, wide rubber band*
• *Scissors • Glue*

What To Do

Measure two 10 cm squares on the paper and your children can cut them out. Roll each square tightly into a thin cylinder and glue in place so they do not unroll. When the glue has dried, bend each cylinder in the middle and then wrap them together with the rubber band around the middle.

Hold one of the cylinders firmly while you wind the other up as tightly as possible. Carefully place the Jumping Jack inside a box or perhaps a book. Ask someone to open it and watch their face!

activity

169

PADDLEPOP CREATIONS

6+

Collect paddlepop sticks or buy them cheaply from craft or junk stores and your kids will love creating all sorts of exciting things from them.

What You Need

- *strong PVA or craft glue*
- *paddlepop sticks*
- *newspaper* • *paint*

What To Do

Spread some newspaper on a table so the glue won't stick and work out what they would like to make. They could make something they could use, like a small box, by laying sticks in a square shape and gradually building it up, or they could simply create something like a plane or an animal. Most children are far more inventive than us 'oldies' and they will have lots of fun making wonderful creations. Just remind them that the glue does dry clear if it looks messy and that PVA and craft glue will need some time to dry. When the creation is dry they will enjoy painting it.

activity
170

PAPIER MACHE BOWLS

6+

My friend Kerenne, a primary school teacher here on the Gold Coast, makes these bowls with the children in her class to give to their Mums for Christmas. A useful and colourful gift idea she has shared with us.

What You Need

- *Picnic set bowl or plate*
- *Newspaper and butcher's paper*
- *Glue (wallpaper paste is excellent)*
- *Acrylic paint*

What To Do

Any shaped bowl or plate can be the basic mould for your children's papier mache creation, but Kerenne prefers to use plastic in case of accidents. Cover the bowl really well with Vaseline before applying the papier mache so it can lift off well when it is dry.

Apply the newspaper in strips. Dip into the wallpaper paste and stick on. Papier mache is a slow process - do a few layers each day.

When the bowl is nearly thick enough, help your children to make the last few layers from strips of white butcher's paper.

When it is all dry, they paint the inside and outside well with white acrylic paint. Kerenne says that large bright designs look great painted on the bowls and she gets the children to draw on their designs, first with a felt pen, then paint after. Maybe your children could colour-co-ordinate the bowl to your kitchen or family room decor for a cheap designer look!

activity
171

PLASTICINE PLAY

6+

A different medium for creating. Cheap to buy but lots of fun.

What You Need

• *Plasticine available from newsagents, school suppliers and toy shops.*

What To Do

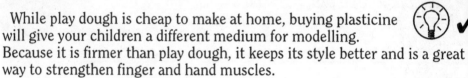

While play dough is cheap to make at home, buying plasticine will give your children a different medium for modelling. Because it is firmer than play dough, it keeps its style better and is a great way to strengthen finger and hand muscles.

It usually comes in a variety of colours too, which adds another interesting dimension to creating. Sit down with your children and show them how to model people, animals and other shapes. They might like to create a whole plasticine environment - a dinosaur landscape or perhaps a farm.

For added interest, pipecleaners, matches, paddlepop sticks, beads, and other things can be used with the plasticine.

activity
172

POTATO MEN

6+

 ✓

 ✓

Potatoes have such interesting shapes they make wonderful 'men!' Show your children how they can do this with a few bits and pieces and lots of imagination.

What You Need

- *large potatoes • toothpicks*
- *small scrubbing brush*
- *playdough or plasticine*
- *bits and pieces to decorate with - lace, felt, fabric scraps, coloured paper, ribbons, lace and so on*

 ✓

What To Do

Give the children a large bowl of warm water and they can begin by scrubbing all the dirt off their potatoes. Next they dry them with a tea towel. Now they are ready to begin making Potato Men.

Help them use the toothpicks (some may have to be shortened) to hold the playdough or plasticine in place for the facial features - eyes, nose, mouth and ears.

Now they can use the fabric, paper and so on to make bow tie, hats and other clothes. Cotton wool dyed black or brown could be the hair or perhaps a moustache. Lady Potato People might like a ribbon or bow in their hair. Help the children make a whole family of Potato People.

When they've finished the project they can scrub some more potatoes for a yummy snack. Show them how to rub the skins with some olive oil and bake in a fairly hot oven. When they are crispy on the outside, and soft in the middle take them out. Cut off the tops, scoop out some of the middle and mix with grated cheese and ham. Pop them back in the oven for a few minutes and then take out.
A very "more-ish" snack or a simple and easy tea.

activity
173

RUBBER BAND BALL

6+

A fun recycling activity that will also help develop your children's fine motor skills.

What You Need

• *Rubber bands*

What To Do

We seem to get rubber bands every day around the papers and the mail and they certainly can accumulate. Recycle them by making rubber band balls with your children. They will love a bouncing ball they made themselves.

Scrunch together a few rubber bands or even tie them and begin stretching the others around this core as many times as necessary. Keep building it until it is the size you want. You can make lots together or your children and their friends might like to have a competition to see who can make the biggest - maybe an item for the Guinness Book of Records!!!

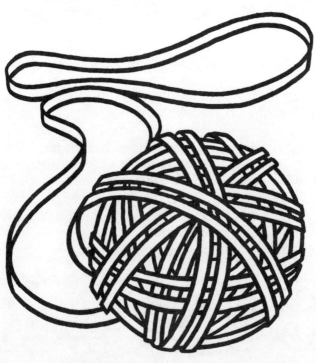

activity
174

STAINED GLASS PICTURES   6+

A way to use up old crayons to create beautiful colourful pictures.

What You Need

- *Old broken wax crayons*
- *Grease proof paper* • *Iron*

What To Do

Help your children grate old wax crayons into separate piles of colours.

They then make a design or picture on the waxed paper with the crayon gratings. Cover this with another piece of waxed paper and iron the two pieces together using a cool iron.

You can frame their creation or just Blu-Tack it on a window where the sun will shine through to give it a 'stained glass' window effect.

activity

175

STAINED GLASS WINDOWS   6+

Another activity with cellophane scraps to help your children learn about colour mixing and making new colours.

What You Need

- *Scissors* • *Glue or sticky tape*
- *Scraps of cellophane* • *Paper*

What To Do

Your children may need help to fold a piece of paper three times. They then cut interesting shapes out of the sides of the paper. Open it up to see what they have made. Now help your children glue or tape pieces of cellophane over the cut out shapes for a very colourful effect. Hang these 'stained glass' pictures on their bedroom windows with the sun shining through. Perhaps you could visit a local church or cathedral so they can see real stained glass windows.

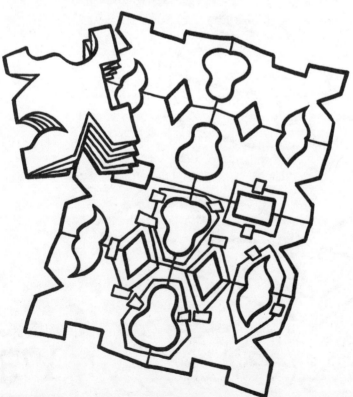

activity
176

STENCILS

6+

Like most people, I buy a lot of the family's meat and chicken on styrofoam trays. Wash these up and save them because they make excellent stencils for the children to paint with.

What You Need

- *styrofoam trays*
- *pencils or pens*
- *scissors or a stanley knife*
- *paints*
- *brushes*
- *paper*

What To Do

Have your children draw a simple design on the trays with a pencil or ball point pen. Use sharp-pointed scissors or a stanley knife to cut out the design. Your children put the stencil over a piece of paper and paint inside the cut-out section. Lift if off carefully and admire their design.

Hint

Make wrapping paper or cards with stencils. Perhaps heart shapes for Valentine's Day cards, bells, trees or holly leaves for Christmas wrapping paper or cards, or balloons for birthday wrapping paper. I'm sure your children will be able to think of lots more great ideas!

activity
177

STREAMERS

6+

Children love making these colourful streamers for sports days, processions, or just to use as dancing props.

What You Need

- *pieces of dowel, rulers, chopsticks or long unsharpened pencils*
- *crepe paper of all colours*
- *strong glue*
- *scissors*

What To Do

Help the children cut out long lengths of crepe paper. Choose a few strips of different colours and glue them from the end of a piece of dowel or ruler, pencil or chopstick. Roll up the streamers tightly and then unwind. Show the children how to wave the streamers around to create colourful displays. They can hold a streamer in each hand and let the colours mix. Put on some dancing music out in the back yard and let the kids dance with their streamers.

Hint

Streamers are great for school Sports Day made in their school or house colours. Volunteer to go to your children's classroom the day before Sports Day, take all the makings and help the children make streamers in their own house colours. You'll be a very popular person.

activity
178

TOOTHPICK MODELS

6+

Children will spend hours modelling with toothpicks and some clay, plasticine and matchsticks. Bring out all these things on those wet, boring days and they will be happily occupied for ages. (Well at least for long enough for you to read the paper and have a cup of coffee!)

What You Need

- *toothpicks (for younger children you could substitute dead matchsticks or the brightly dyed matchsticks available at craft or junk stores.)*
- *plasticine, clay or playdough*

What To Do

Show the children how to roll small balls of the plasticine, playdough or clay and then stick the toothpicks in them. Use the balls as the corner stones of the houses and other buildings they make. They can stick in lots of toothpicks to form the walls and then make doors, windows, and roofs out of pieces of paper or cardboard.

Bring out some small props and they could make farms for their farm animals, houses for Lego or Duplo people or perhaps an airport or bridge for small planes and cars. They'll think of lots of creative ways to use the toothpicks once you get them started.

Don't forget to find the camera to take some photos of their wonderful creations before they fall to pieces. Who knows - you may have an architect in the family one day!

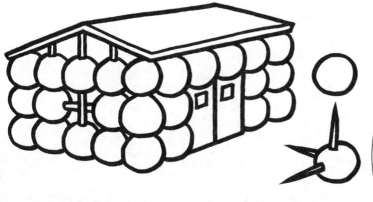

activity
179

TREASURE CHESTS 6+

Children love having special little boxes in which to store treasured possessions. Show your children how simply they can be made out of household junk.

What You Need

- *Empty tetra-pak juice containers* • *Sticky tape*
- *Stanley knife or scissors* • *A ruler and a pen*
- *Paint and other materials for decoration*

What To Do

Decide together with the children how large they want their special box to be. Measure the distance from the bottom of the juice container and draw a cutting line with the ruler and pen. Cut along the two sides of the pack and the front at this point, but not the back.

Next, form the lid from the remaining long piece at the back of the box. Measure the depth and width of the box, add them together (older children can do this - it's great maths practice), and mark this on the lid flap. Cut carefully and then bend the lid over in the appropriate places.

Your children will enjoy decorating their own special box. They can begin by painting it - household paints work well, or acrylic paints - and then decorate the boxes with glitter, sequins, bits of ribbon, lace or fabric offcuts, pretty flowers or leaves from the garden, pictures cut from greeting cards or magazines or their own art work.

To keep the box closed, use some adhesive velcro (available from sewing shops) or a button and a loop at the front.

activity
180

TWIG WEAVINGS

6+

Introduce your children to the concept of weaving with this fun activity.

What You Need

- *Twigs about 30cm - 40cm long*
- *Pieces of wool, ribbon, strips of fabric, etc.*
- *Something to hang it from*
- *Sharp knife*

What To Do

Explain the concept of warps and weft to your children. Together look at some loosely woven fabric such as hessian or linen so they understand.

Cut about 20 pieces of wool of equal length for the warp. With the knife, cut notches in the sticks at equal distances so the wool doesn't slide. Tie the warp threads to the bottom and top sticks and, with another piece of wool, hang it to a door handle, a hook or a tree branch.

Anchor the bottom stick to a brick so it stays steady while your children are weaving. Your children then use the rest of the wool or other materials to make an interesting weaving.

Later, they can cut the weaving off to use as a mat or hang it up in the frame.

activity
181

WET CHALK DRAWINGS

6+

Soak sticks of coloured chalk in water to provide a different drawing medium for your children.

What You Need

- *Coloured chalk sticks* • *Water*
- *Paper (if you want to spend a little money, buy some black paper - the effect is terrific)*

What To Do

Your children can help you soak the chalk sticks in water for about ten minutes. Warn them not to press too hard as they draw because the chalk can break easily.

Drawing with wet chalk on black paper looks especially effective, but it's just as interesting on white.

Happy drawing!

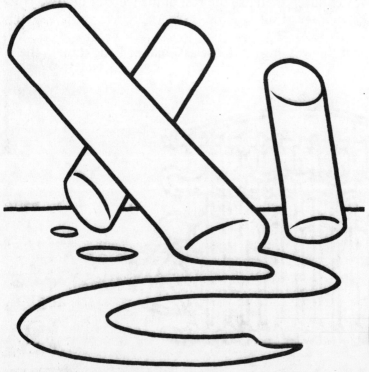

activity
182

BATH FIZZ!

8+

 ✓

 ✓

Help your children make some deliciously scented bath salts to use or give away as gifts. Add some excitement to bath time!

What You Need

 ✓

- Bicarbonate of soda
- Cornflour
- Cream of tartar
- Essential oils such as lavender (available from Health Food Stores))
- A glass bottle with a lid
- A measuring cup

What To Do

Measure three-quarters of a cup of bicarbonate of soda, two tablespoons of cornflour and half a cup of cream of tartar. Put them all into the jar and stir well to mix and break up any lumps.

Add a few drops of an essential oil or perfume and mix really well again.

When your children are in the bath, drop in spoonfuls of the Bath Salts and they will enjoy the fizzy sensation and the delicious smell.

activity
183

BOX PUPPETS

8+

Help your kids make a marionette puppet that works really well out of household junk.

 ✓

 ✓

What You Need

- *A milk carton • Paper • String*
- *Felt pens and other materials to decorate the puppet*
- *Glue • Sticks • A pencil*

 ✓

What To Do

Help your kids make a hole in each side of the top part of the milk carton for the puppet's arms. To make movable arms, wrap strips of paper tightly around a pencil and then glue the strips in place. Thread a long piece of string through the milk carton and then thread the paper cylinders onto the string to make arms on each side. Next tie more strings onto the arms and attach to sticks that make the puppet work. Next make two legs in the same way.

The children will enjoy decorating the milk carton and finally attaching a string to the top of the milk carton to make the 'head' move.

Tie the crossed sticks together and make the puppet move by moving the sticks.

Help them make a few marionette puppets and put on a puppet show together.

activity

184

CITRUS PEEL JEWELLERY   8+

Help your children make some creative and individual jewellery from citrus fruit to give as gifts or for themselves.

What You Need

- *Oranges, lemons, grapefruit, mandarins, limes*
- *String or leather thonging*
- *Sharp knife*
- *Pencil or knitting needle*

What To Do

Help your children cut interesting shapes from the citrus peel. (Eat the rest of the fruit or make some delicious juice).

Make holes in each piece while it is still soft and leave to dry. Flatten some pieces by leaving a weight on them while they are drying. Make cylindrical pieces by winding strips around the pencil or knitting needle.

When they are all dry, your children can thread them onto string or the leather thonging. Make the designs different by alternating small beads (available from bead or craft shops).

activity
185

COLOURFUL BOTTLES

8+

Your children will love your help to make these colourful bottles. They make useful and decorative storage, look great just for display, or give them away for gifts.

What You Need

- *Bottles of different shapes and sizes*
- *Metallic spray paints (available from hardware and craft stores)*
- *Masking tape*
- *Scissors*
- *Newspaper*

What To Do

Help your children cut out shapes from the masking tape and use them to decorate the bottles. Stars, moons, hearts, fish, shells, flowers and geometric shapes all look great.

Next, spread an area well with newspaper and help them carefully spray the bottles. When they are dry, peel off the masking to reveal the interesting patterns they have made.

Help them name their work (like all artists) by writing their name on the bottom of their bottle art!

activity

186

DOT PAINTINGS

8+

To encourage colour awareness and an appreciation of art in your children.

What You Need

- *Drawing paper (eg. computer paper, etc.)*
- *Paints and a fine brush (only primary colours)*
- *Coloured pencils (red, blue, yellow)*
- *Fine pointed felt pens*

What To Do

Encourage your children to draw or paint using only a technique of tiny dots of primary colours. Your children may prefer to use a lead pencil to lightly pencil in the drawing and then colour it with the dots.

Show your children some Impressionist paintings that use this technique, eg. Vincent Van Gogh, Seurat, Monet and others. Your local library will have lots of art books you can borrow to look at with your children, or perhaps you are lucky enough to live in a city/town with an Art Gallery you can visit together.

As your children can only use dots of primary colours, they will have to think carefully about what dots to mix together to produce other colours, perhaps yellow and red to produce orange.

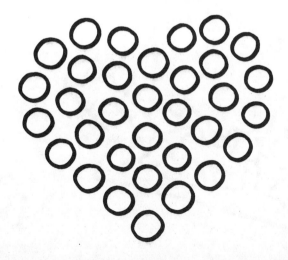

activity
187

ETCHINGS

Older children will love this new way to make colourful drawings.

What You Need

- *Paper*
- *Crayons or craypas*
- *Match sticks, spoons, broken pencils*

What To Do

Show your children how to fill a whole piece of paper with every colour crayon except black. It is important that this first layer of colour is quite thick, so make sure your children press down heavily and apply the colour all over. Next, take a black crayon and, using it on its side, cover all the colours with black.

Then show the children how to use a pointed implement such as spoon handle, paint brush end or match stick, to scratch a picture on the paper. The black is scratched away, leaving the bright colours revealed.

activity
188

GOD'S EYES

8+

Show your children how to make this simple form of folk art.   They originated in South America and were religious symbols.

 ✓

 ✓

What You Need

- *Brightly coloured wool*
- *Two sticks about 15-20cm long*

 ✓

What To Do

 ✓

 Hold the sticks while your children tie them together to form a cross. You then show them how to hold the two sticks together where they join and loop the wool around the first stick close to the knot.   Wrap the wool first around one stick, then the next, to keep forming X's.   Remind them to keep turning the god's eye as they work.

 Change wool often, tying one colour to the next to make it as bright as possible.   Finish the god's eye off by tying the wool to the stick.

 Bells and tassels are often added to make them even more colourful and decorative.

 Your children might like to make a few to decorate a wall in their bedroom.

activity
189

INSERT BROOCHES

8+

Older children with some basic sewing skills will enjoy making some insect brooches to decorate a plain sweatshirt or T-shirt or to give to special friends as a gift.

What You Need

- *Oddments of felt and lace*
- *Safety pins*
- *Old pantihose*
- *Sequins*
- *Felt pen*
- *Chalk*
- *Mug*
- *Craft glue*
- *Scissors*
- *Needle and thread*

What To Do

Begin by making a ladybird. Draw a small circle on some red or orange felt or fabric and help your children cut it out. Show them how to sew large running stitches as close to the edge of the fabric as possible. Next, help them gather up the running stitches and put some pieces of cut-up pantihose in the centre. Pull the stitches up really tight and tie off the ends. Mould it into a long oval shape and sew carefully over the gap to close it.

Your children will enjoy marking on the ladybird's spots with a black felt pen. Add a safety pin to attach it.

To make a bee, follow the same steps using black felt or black fabric. Then glue on with the craft glue some strips of yellow felt to make the bee's stripes. Some scraps of lace make great wings and again attach a safety pin at the back.

To make a butterfly brooch, use purple or pink felt or fabric and add some beautiful lacy wings and glue on some bright sequins. Again, add a safety pin at the back for attaching.

activity

190

KNOCK KNOCK CARDS

8+

Help your children make their own joke cards to give to their friends. Lots of creative fun and saves money too!

What You Need

- *Paper* • *Scissors*
- *Stanley knife*
- *Glue* • *Felt Pens*

What To Do

Measure together two blank pieces of paper about 20 cm by 14 cm. Your children cut them out carefully and then fold each one in half.

Draw a square about 5 cm by 5 cm on the front of one of the cards and then cut it out on three sides so it opens like a door. It is easier to cut this with a Stanley knife, but if your children want to do it all themselves, start off the cut with the cutting knife and let them do the rest with scissors.

Next, glue the uncut card to the inside of this card, except where the window is. When it is dry your children can decorate the card with a Knock-Knock joke and put the answer inside the card.

activity
191

LET'S MODEL

8+

A great way for older children to make models that last for ever.

What You Need

- *Plaster of Paris*
  (available from hardware stores or craft suppliers)
- *Plain flour*
- *Water* • *Paint*

What To Do

Your children can help you make up a modelling mixture using one part Plaster of Paris, three parts of flour and enough water to make a dough consistency.

This mixture will remain workable for about an hour. Your children will enjoy making models with the mixture. Dry them in the sun until very firm and then the children can paint them.

Who knows, they may become sculptors one day!

activity
192

MODELLING DOUGH

8+

This simply-made dough is good for making small jewellery and ornaments.

What You Need

- *White bread*
- *Glue*
- *Lemon juice or eucalyptus oil*

What To Do

Cut off the crusts from half a dozen slices of the bread and break into little pieces. Add two tablespoons of glue and the juice of half a lemon or a few drops of eucalyptus oil.

Mix it all thoroughly until it is ready for your children to use for modelling.

Making beads is a simple activity but make sure any holes are made before the object dries.

Place the finished pieces on a tray covered with grease proof paper.

The dough items will take at least two days to dry and should be turned frequently.

Later your children will enjoy painting their creation with some acrylic or water paints.

activity
193

ORANGE POMANDERS

8+

Revive an old-fashioned craft by making fragrant pomander balls with your children.

What You Need

- *Oranges with thin skins*
- *Cloves* • *Ribbon*
- *1 tablespoon of cinnamon*
- *1 tablespoon of orris powder (available from chemists)*
- *Skewer or thin kebab stick*
- *Paper bag*
- *issue paper or kitchen wrap paper*

What To Do

Show the children how to make holes in the oranges with the skewers. Make holes all over and then insert a clove in each hole. Do this until the orange is totally covered with cloves.

Then, help the children combine the cinnamon and orris powder in a paper bag, and shake the oranges in the mixture until they are quite powdery. Wrap the oranges in the tissue paper and leave for a month. Leave them in a warm place, and in a month they will be ready.

They look great tied with Christmas ribbon.

Grandmas and Aunts will love one for a gift to hang in their cupboards!

activity
194

PAPIER MACHE

8+

A long term project for older children that has heaps of uses!

What You Need

 ✓

• *Non-toxic wallpaper paste* • *Balloon*
• *Strips of newspaper about 4 cm wide*

 ✓

What To Do

Blow up the balloon and simply dip strips of newspaper into the wallpaper paste and place on the balloon.

Papier mache must be done slowly and allowed to dry well between each application so it won't mildew. Don't apply more than three or four layers at a time. Peg the balloon on the clothesline so it dries quickly. When the papier mache is strong enough, burst the balloon inside with a pin and it can be cut and used for something special.

Make some masks out of your papier mache or a collection of funny animals.

activity
195

SHOE BOX DIORAMA

8+

A special way to display small objects or make a favourite story come to life.

What You Need

• *A shoe box* • *Playdough, plasticine or Blu-tack*
• *Ice block sticks*

What To Do

Help your children cut out the side of the shoe box. Decide what scene you are going to make and think of what you can use.

They could paint the sides and back of the shoe box first with colours suitable for the scene they are going to make.

Small mirrors or cellophane make excellent ponds, crepe paper can be used for trees and grass. Ice block sticks can be decorated for people and the play dough, plasticine or Blu-Tack can hold objects in place.

Your children may like to make a farm, a dinosaur world or perhaps their favourite fairy tale or nursery rhyme!

activity
196

STABILES

8+

Stabiles are lots of fun to make.

 ✓

What You Need

 ✓

- *Clay, plasticine or polystyrene for the base*
- *Toothpicks, ice block sticks, pipe cleaners, pasta, polystyrene pieces, leaves, flowers*
- *Coloured paper or cardboard*
- *Sticky tape or Blu-Tack*

 ✓

What To Do

 ✓

Using the clay, plasticine or a piece of polystyrene as a base, your children poke the sticks, pipe cleaners or toothpicks into it.

They then decorate them with leaves, flowers or shapes. If they need to secure them, use small blobs of Blu-Tack or sticky tape.

Fun to make at Christmas time also, using pictures cut from old cards, bits of tinsel and small decorations. Make one with your children for a centrepiece for the Christmas dinner table.

activity
197

T-SHIRT ART

8+

Your children will proudly wear a T-shirt that they have decorated themselves.

What You Need

- *Plain T-shirt*
- *Fabric crayons (available at fabric and craft shops)*
- *White paper* • *Iron and ironing board* • *Tea towel*

What To Do

Suggest to your children that they work out their design before drawing it with the fabric crayons. When they have done that, they draw the design on the white paper, colouring as heavily as they can.

Put a tea towel on the ironing board and pull the front of the T-shirt through the board. (This will stop the design going through to the other side of the T-shirt).

Place the drawing face down on the fabric and do the ironing yourself. Press down with a warm iron all over the design (don't move the iron back and forward or the design will blur). The crayon picture will transfer to the T-shirt.

Remove the piece of paper and see how the wax has melted the design onto the T-shirt.

Your children may like to decorate the back of their T-shirt also!

activity
198

DRY FOOD JEWELLERY

10+

Older children will enjoy making unusual jewellery from dried foods. A cheap new trend!

What You Need

- *Dried fruit, such as dried apple rings*
- *Dried beans*
- *Macaroni*
- *Needle and thread*
- *Clear varnish and a brush*
- *Paper clips*

What To Do

Help your children work out a pattern with the dried fruit, beans and macaroni. Then they carefully sew through the dried fruit, the macaroni and, last, the beans.

When the necklace is finished, help them attach a paper clip to each end so they can link together to fasten the necklace.

Your children can even make matching earrings and a bracelet.

The varnish adds to the appearance as well as making the jewellery last longer too.

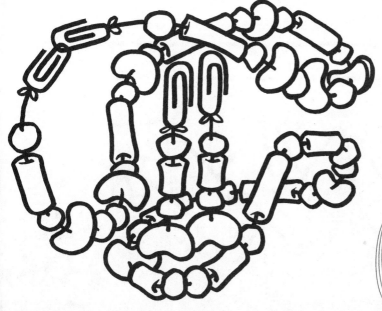

activity
199

PAPER JEWELLERY

10+

Older children will enjoy creating their own jewellery from colourful paper to match an outfit for a special event.

What You Need

• *Colourful paper - can be bought from the newsagents, but old wrapping paper, advertising brochures, envelope insides and brown paper work well too.*

What To Do

To make a colourful bracelet, take two long strips of contrasting paper. Glue the ends together at right angles and then fold one piece over the other, then over the other and so on. (Your children will probably have made Christmas streamers using this method). Glue the ends together when it is finished. This bracelet expands like a concertina so the children will be able to slip it over an arm easily.

Make a matching necklace by cutting long, thin paper triangles. Begin with the wide end and roll the triangle as tightly as possible around a pencil or knitting needles. Put a spot of glue at the end to hold it in place. Thread the colourful beads onto some wool or cord.

Instant chic!

activity
200

PASTA PHOTO FRAMES

10+ ✓

Help your children make some interesting photo frames for their room or to give as gifts.

What You Need

 ✓

- *Strong cardboard*
- *Strong glue such as Craft Glue or Aquadhere*
- *Variety of pasta shapes (bows, twirls, etc.)*
- *Gold or silver metallic spray paint*

What To Do

 ✓

Select the photos first for size, then cut a piece of strong card to double the size you need, with room for a border. Score with a knife and ruler and then fold in half carefully. Cut out the section for the photo, leaving a border of at least 4 cm (although the 'in' look for frames now is to have a much wider border!).

Help your children decorate the frame with the pasta shapes and strong glue. Leave to dry. If you wish, spray with the gold or silver paint, but make sure you do this outside on a still day.

Glue the photo in the frame and glue together. Attach a small piece of strong card at the back so your frame can stand up.

activity
201

POMPOMS

10+

Older children will be able to make lots of small animals once they have mastered the knack of making woollen pompoms.

What You Need

- *Scissors* • *Needle and cotton*
- *Wool* • *Cardboard*
- *Strong glue such as Aquadhere*

What To Do

Help your children cut two round circles from cardboard - whatever size they want the finished pompoms to be. Next, cut a small hole in the centre of each cardboard circle. Your children then wrap wool around and around the circles until the centre hole is completely full.

With the point of the scissors, they cut the wool between the two circles. Take a length of wool and help your children tie it between the circles and knot firmly. Then they cut away the cardboard, trim the tie and are left with a pompom.

They could join lots of pompoms together to make a caterpillar, make a pompom teddy or mouse, or attach it to hat elastic and a paper cup and use it for a catch game. Pompoms also make great decorations on hats and clothes.

activity
202

MATHS IS FUN

CLOTHES PEG SORTING

2+

A simple colour sorting game to play with your children. Sorting colours is the first step in learning to name them.

What You Need

• *Plastic clothes pegs of different colours*
• *Ice cream containers*

What To Do

Have a container for each colour peg. Clip a different coloured peg onto the side of each container.

Your children will then enjoy sorting the pegs by colour into the correct container. When they have finished this, show them how to clip the pegs around the side of the container. (This will be difficult for some children, but persist over time as they need strong finger muscles to begin writing.)

Later, you can help them count which container holds the most pegs. Can they name their colours yet? See which ones they are not sure of and play colour-learning games together as you dress, bath and play with them through the day.

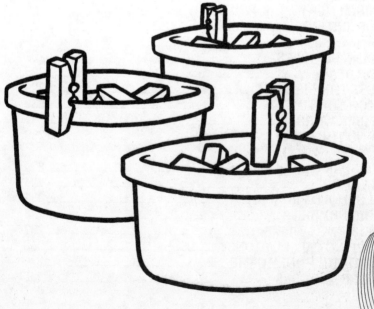

activity
203

FISHING FUN

2+

A fun way to practise counting and to make size comparisons.

What You Need

- *ruler or a short length of dowel*
- *string* • *magnet* • *paper clips*
- *coloured cardboard* • *scissors*

What To Do

Cut out lots of cardboard fish. Be imaginative and make them different shapes, sizes and colours. Slide a paper clip onto each fish's "mouth". Tie a magnet onto the ruler or length of dowel with some string. Your children will love catching the "fish" and telling you about them. Ask them to show you all the red fish, or all the blue or green fish. Next see if they can show you the largest or smallest fish. Talk about all the colours and do lots of counting.

Follow up the fishing game with fish and chips for tea!

activity
204

GARAGES

2+

Learning how to sort objects into sizes is an important mathematical skill. This activity will help teach your young children how to do this in a fun play way.

What You Need

• *toy cars of various sizes*
• *boxes of various sizes*

What To Do

Match the boxes to the sizes of the cars or else cut doorways in the boxes to fit the different sized cars.

our children will have lots of fun driving the cars into the right garages. See if they can order the cars from the smallest to the largest. Practise counting how many cars there are altogether too!

activity
205

LARGE AND SMALL

2+

 ✓
 ✓

 ✓
✓

An activity to help younger children begin to sort and classify.

What You Need
- *Large and small boxes, e.g. apple box, shoe box*
- *Big and small versions of the same objects, e.g.*

large toy car	*small match box car*
large comb	*small comb*
large brush	*small brush*
tablespoon	*teaspoon*
large stone	*small stone*
large leaf	*small leaf*

What To Do

Place all the items you have found on a tray. Your children find an item, then its smaller or larger version, and then puts them into the correct boxes, i.e. small items in the shoe box, large ones in the apple box.

Talk lots about big and little or large and small in everyday situations with your young children. Fun play situations like this are the way young children learn.

big

small

activity
206

MATCHING GAMES

2+

Make sure your children have lots of opportunities to try matching objects - this is an important mathematical step.

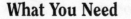

What You Need   *Find lots of objects to match :*
- *pair of socks*
- *clothes pegs*
- *buttons*
- *toys*
- *shoes*
- *cutlery*
- *gloves*

What To Do

Simply collect all the pairs in a large box and have your children look through it to find all the pairs.

Your children will enjoy helping you sort the washing, and also finding everyone's pairs of socks.

activity
207

OUTLINES

2+

An activity to help younger children learn to compare size and to order according to size.

What You Need

• *Paper* • *Pencil*

What To Do

Have your children place their hand down on a piece of paper and spread their fingers. Trace around the outline of their hand. Help them cut it out.

Now do the same to your own hand and other members of the family so your children can compare them and then put them in size sequence. Talk about bigger than and smaller than.

Do the same with the family's feet (after they have bathed or showered!). Your children might have fun putting out the footprint line to follow.

Keep their hand and foot outlines so you can compare them with new ones in a year or so. You'll be amazed at how much they've grown.

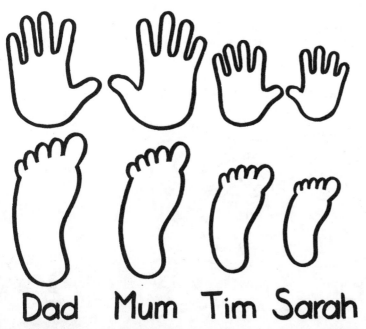

Dad   Mum   Tim   Sarah

activity
208

POURING AND MEASURING   2+

A fun activity which can be extended to a measuring activity for older children.

What You Need

- *A sheet, table cloth or small clean tarp*
- *A large plastic tub*
- *Mixture of rice*
- *Any or all of the following - different sorts of pasta eg. shells, tubes, macaroni and spirals, rolled oats, sago, dried beans.*

What To Do

Spread out the sheet on the family room floor, fill the tub and let them go. Provide toys from your children's sandpit as well as funnels, cups, spoons of different sizes, strainers and jugs.

As well as simply enjoying playing in and manipulating the material, your children may enjoy using trucks, cars, diggers and animals in the tub. The different mixtures make great loads for small trucks and backhoes.

Encourage your children to create mountains, valleys and other interesting landscapes for toy animals, or even a moonscape or dinosaur world.

Make sure the tub is securely covered after playing or better still transferred to larger sealed containers to discourage vermin sharing the fun.

activity
209

SORTING TIME

2+

 ✓
 ✓

Sorting things into groups or sets is a very early basic mathematical skill. As your toddlers help you sort the washing they are gaining important sorting skills.

What You Need

• *washing to sort*

 ✓

What To Do

Sort out the family's washing on your bed so there's plenty of room to spread out. Work out together where each person's pile will be. Encourage your young children to verbalise, "That's where we put Daddy's things" and "My things go here".

Then your children can help you put the items in the correct piles and find pairs of socks. When all the sorting is completed they can help carry each person's pile to their bedroom.

activity
210

ZANY MATCH-UPS

2+

A fun matching game you can make yourself for younger children.

What You Need

- *Collect a variety of small items such as:*
  comb, bobby pin, pencil, pen, spoon, knife, screwdriver, pegs, rubber bands, safety pin, scissors, buttons, small blocks, match box, cotton reel, small pins
- *A large sheet of cardboard* • *Contact*
- *Small box or container for the objects*
- *Fine, coloured felt pens or coloured pencils*

What To Do

Trace around the objects; if they are coloured, use the same colour for the outline. Keep all the objects in a container for matching. Cover the cardboard with contact to keep it clean.

Your children match the objects to the outlines. Ask them questions such as:

How many red things are there?
How many are made from metal?
Can you find me something that's made from plastic?

Later they might like you to time them to see how fast they can match the objects or see if they can beat an egg-timer.

activity
211

BIG FEET

4+

Another fun mathematics activity that helps your young children compare sizes and learn mathematical terms such as largest, smallest and bigger than and smaller than.

What You Need

• *Plastic ice-cream container lids or strong cardboard*
• *Elastic* • *Felt pen*

What To Do

Draw around your own feet (or your husband's). Cut out the feet and attach elastic so your children can discover what it's like to have BIG FEET.

When you are walking on the beach or in the sandpit compare all the family's footprints. Can they tell you who has the largest feet, the smallest etc.?

activity
212

BUTTONS

A sorting game which helps your children work out similarities and differences for themselves.

What You Need

- *Lots of assorted buttons in a container*
- *Egg cartons or ice cube trays*

What To Do

If you don't have lots of different sized, shape and colour buttons in your button box, charity shops such as Life Line and St Vincent de Paul's always have them for sale for a small price.

Give them to your children to sort out according to their own criteria first.   Ask them to explain to you what they have done.

If they are having difficulty with this, offer some suggestions such as:

- Could you sort them out into different colours?
- Could you find all the ones with two holes in first and then the ones with four holes?
- Could you put all the metal ones together?

For younger children who are having difficulties matching colours, colour the bottom of an egg carton with different colours and your children sort the buttons into the correct hole.

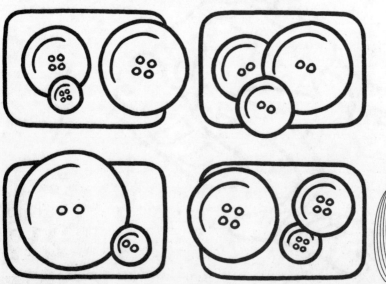

activity
213

ENVIRONMENTAL NUMBER CHART 4+

Go for a walk around the garden or to a local park and collect lots of interesting leaves, seeds, flowers, gumnuts, twigs, small pebbles, grasses and other materials to make an environmental number chart with your children.

What You Need

- *Large sheet of thick cardboard*
- *Strong glue (PVA)*
- *Brush*
- *Felt Pens*
- *Environmental materials*

What To Do

When you come home from your walk, your children can sort out all the things you have collected into groups.   Draw up a number chart together (see below).

Help them glue on the correct number of items beside each numeral.   This way they will learn to match the numeral with the number of objects.

Hang it in a special spot in their bedroom and practise counting together before they go to sleep each night.

Andrews Number Chart	
1	🥚
2	❀ ❀
3	⟋ ⟍
4	🍃 🍃 🍃 🍃
5	△ △ △ △ △
6	○ ○ ○ ○ ○ ○

activity
214

ESTIMATION

4+

Estimating and trying to guess what is going to happen next is an important aspect of mathematics and science. Develop your children's powers of estimation by asking them questions like those listed below.

What You Need

- *Building blocks*
- *Large jug of water*
- *Measuring cups*
- *Egg timer*
- *Marbles in a container*
- *Hammer, nails, and a block of wood*

What To Do

Use the materials above and pose questions to your children, such as:

- How many blocks do you think you can build up into a tower before they will fall?
- How many yellow blocks do you think you will need to lay them end to end right across the doorway?
- How many cups of water do you think you will need to fill up the jug?
- How many marbles do you think you will need to fill a measuring cup?
- How many times do you think you will have to bang the nail with the hammer to hammer it right into the piece of wood?
- How many times do you think we will have to turn the egg-timer before you have tidied your room, put away that game, or picked up those blocks?

After your children have given you their estimations, work them out together and see how close they were.

activity

215

MY DAY

4+

Young children find learning to tell the time very difficult. Before they can understand, they must acquire a sense of event sequence. Activities like 'My Day' will help.

What You Need

• *A long strip of paper* • *Felt pens or coloured pencils*

What To Do

Discuss with your children the sorts of things they would do in a normal day.

Begin by suggesting to your children they draw a sun at one end of the paper and the moon and stars at the other, for the beginning and end of their day. Next, they draw in their day - when they get up, have breakfast, get dressed, go to preschool, things they do there, come home, play outside, have their bath, have dinner, play or watch TV, brush their teeth, have stories, go to bed. Hang their 'My Day' picture in their bedroom and talk about it together.

Hang a calendar in their room and if they are looking forward to a particular event, perhaps a birthday party or having a friend sleep over, together you can cross off the days as they pass.

Children need to have a good grasp of the sequence of daily events and days before they can tell the time from a clock.

activity
216

MY WEEK

4+

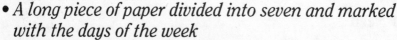
Help your children understand more about the passing of time and learn the days of the week with this activity.

 ✓

 ✓

What You Need

 ✓

- *A long piece of paper divided into seven and marked with the days of the week*
- *Felt pens or coloured pencils*

 ✓

What To Do

Start the week on a Sunday. Discuss the days of the week with your children as you write their names on the paper. Talk about things you do regularly on certain days:

On Mondays you come to tennis with Mum
On Wednesday you go to kindy
On Saturday Dad takes you to gym classes

At the end of each day have your children draw in the space the things they enjoyed doing most on that day.

At the end of the week hang it in their bedroom and talk about it together using language like 'yesterday', 'tomorrow', 'last week', 'next week', 'night', 'day' and so on.

activity
217

NUMBER MATCH

4+

A simple activity to help young children learn numerals.

What You Need

• *Paper* • *Coloured felt pen*

What To Do

Write lots of numeral pairs 1-5 all over a piece of paper. Your children have to draw lines to match up a pair of numerals the same. Make it even harder by drawing the numerals in different colours - a blue 5 and a yellow 5, a green 3 and a pink 3.

Can they tell you what the numerals are called? Can they find three yellow objects in his room? Five blue pegs in the peg basket? Two green leaves in the garden?

Turn counting and learning numerals into lots of fun. When they know their numerals to 5 add 6 to 10 also.

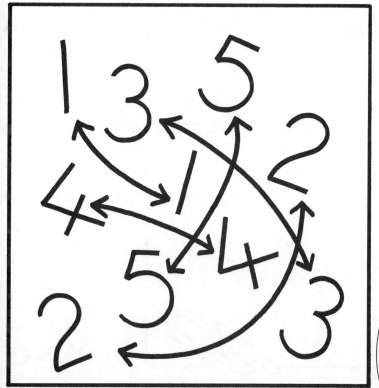

activity
218

PAPER CLIP COUNTING

4+

A fun, hands-on counting game to help children learn numbers.

What You Need

- *10 pieces of cardboard about 12cm square*
- *Felt pens*
- *Paper clips or clothes pegs*

What To Do

Number each of the pieces of cardboard from 1 to 10. Put the corresponding number of dots on each piece of cardboard so your children can count the dots if they cannot yet recognize numerals.

See if your children can slide the correct number of paper clips onto each piece of cardboard. When they are finished check to see if they are right. Older children could play this game with numbers to 20 or higher.

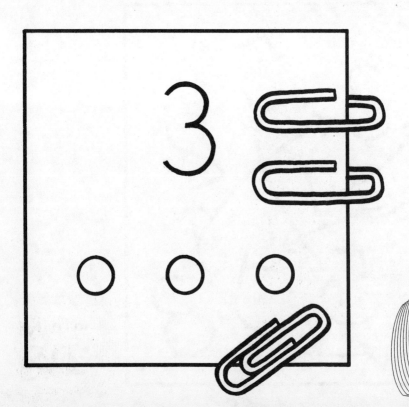

activity
219

SHAPE MOBILES

4+

Help your children learn geometric shapes in a fun way with this balancing activity.

What You Need

- *Stiff cardboard or polystyrene trays*
- *Sticky tape • Scissors • String*
- *Wire coat hangers*

What To Do

Help your children draw and cut out simple geometric shapes - circles, squares, rectangles and triangles. Cut two exactly the same of each shape.

At this stage, they may like to paint, collage or draw on the shapes to decorate them.

Next, cut a slit to the centre of each one and join them at right angles (use the sticky tape to hold them in place).

Your children will enjoy hanging up the shapes in their room on a wire coat hanger. A shape mobile - watch them move and spin in the breeze.

activity
220

WEIGHING

4+

Activities like these will help your children learn about weight and understand terms such as 'lighter than' or 'heavier than'.

What You Need

- *Bathroom scales*
- *Kitchen scales*
- *Various items to measure*
- *Paper/pencil*

What To Do

Begin by measuring all the members of your family. Your children might like to draw a picture of each one and then help them write beside the pictures their weight in kilograms. Discuss who is the heaviest and who is the lightest.

Next, raid the pantry and find tins and packets of various shapes and weights. Let them weigh them and together work out which are the heaviest and which are the lightest. Try to find items that weigh the same but are different shapes or sizes, perhaps a tin of baked beans and a packet of flour.

activity

221

CALCULATOR FUN 6+

Teach your younger children to be familiar and comfortable with simple calculators with fun activities like these.

What You Need

- *A simple cheap calculator (if you are buying one, get one with number keys as large as possible)*
- *Pencils*   *Papers*

What To Do

Show your children how to press the numbers and how to make them disappear. Show them what keys like + and - do.

Next, write some numbers on the paper for them to copy - 4792, 0876, 5398, or 6748. See if they can press the numbers from 1 - 10, or perhaps 1 - 20. Call out numbers and see if they can press them correctly on the calculator - 5, 8, 12, 17, and so on.

Let them also have lots of time to play with and explore their calculator in their own way. When you have things to work out with the calculator, involve them so they can see new ways to use it. Take it grocery shopping with you and show them how to work out the bargains too!

activity
222

DOLLAR DICE

6+

Save all your spare 5 and 10 cent coins to play this counting game with the family.

What You Need

• *A dice*
• *Lots of 5 and 10 cent coins*

What To Do

All the coins are kept in a dish in the middle of the players. The players take it in turn to roll the dice and then take as many coins as is shown on the dice. For example - if you roll a 4 you can take 4 coins out of the dish. It is up to the players whether they take 5 or 10 cent coins.

The amounts are added up as you go and the goal of the game is to be the player who gets as close to a dollar as possible without going over the dollar! The other limit of the game is not to go over 7 rolls of the dice.

(Explain to the children that while it is alright to take 10 cent coins for your first couple of rolls of the dice, it is better after that to take a mixture of 5 cent coins or you will quickly 'break' by going over the dollar.)

activity
223

NAUGHTY THREES

6+

A simple dice game all the family will enjoy.

What You Need

- *2 or more players*
- *Two dice*
- *Paper and pencil*

What To Do

Elect someone to keep the scores first. The game is simple and the first player to reach fifty (or any other designated number) is the winner.

Players take it in turns to throw both dice and only score when two identical numbers are thrown (two 1s, two 2s and so on). All doubles score five points, except for a pair of 6s which scores 25, and a pair of 'Naughty' 3s, which wipes out the player's total score and they then have to start again!

activity
224

NUMBER HUNT

6+

A good game to play as you cook dinner to get the children out from under your feet.

What You Need

• *Time*

What To Do

Call out a number, then ask the children to find objects that represent that number from around the house. For example, a fork has four tines, so that is four; or a rolling pin has two handles - 2; or a chair has four legs - 4.

You will be amazed at how inventive they become.

activity **225**

ODDS AND EVENS

6+

A fun, fast game to play with your children.

What You Need

• *2 players* • *Paper for scoring*

What To Do

You and your children must clench your right fist. Together, count to three and on three each person extends either one or two fingers. As you extend your fingers, you must take it in turn to say 'odds' or 'evens'. If the players extend one finger it is 'evens'; if one extends one and others two, it is, of course, 'odds'.

If a player guesses correctly, they score a point and have another turn at calling. When they guess wrongly, it is the other player's turn to call again. Before you begin the game, decide when it will end - perhaps the first to 20, or maybe when the clock gets to the hour.

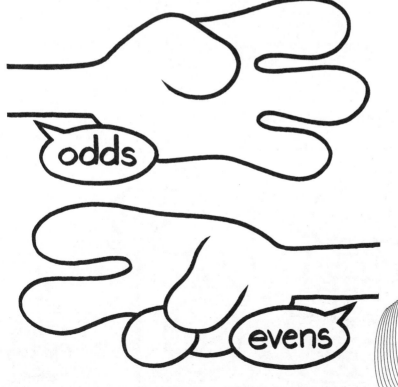

activity
226

ADDING UP HOLES

8+

Improve your children's adding ability as well as their throwing skills with this activity.

What You Need

- *Large cardboard box or piece of strong cardboard*
- *Stanley knife* • *Blackboard or paper to score*
- *Felt pen* • *Tennis ball*

What To Do

On one side of the box or on the cardboard draw five or six holes. Make the smallest one just large enough for the tennis ball to go through. Cut out the holes carefully. Above each hole write the score; the smaller the hole, the larger the score.

Prop up the cardboard or stand the box with the holes towards the players, who then take it in turn to try to throw the ball through the holes. If a ball goes through a hole, write that number beside the player's name.

Improve your children's adding abilities by making them keep a running total. The person with the highest score after a set number of throws is the winner.

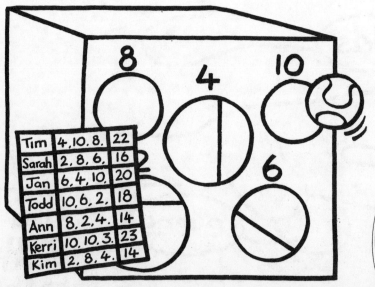

Tim	4, 10. 8.	22
Sarah	2. 8. 6.	16
Jan	6. 4. 10.	20
Todd	10. 6. 2.	18
Ann	8. 2. 4.	14
Kerri	10. 10. 3.	23
Kim	2. 8. 4.	14

activity
227

DROP DEAD

8+

A fun and exciting family dice game.

What You Need

- *2 or more players*
- *Five dice*
- *Paper and pencil to record the scores*

What To Do

The aim of 'Drop Dead' is to make the highest possible score at one turn.

The first player begins by throwing all five dice. Each time they make a throw that does not contain a 2 or a 5, they add together the total number of that throw. They then have another throw. If they do throw a 2 or a 5, they score nothing for that throw and the dice that showed a 2 or a 5 is removed from their turn. A player's turn continues until the last dice shows a 2 or a 5 and they have to 'drop dead' and the next player has their turn.

See who can make the highest score from an individual turn or add up all the scores for the highest total score.

activity
228

GUESS THE DISTANCE

8+

A good game to fill in those tedious times in the car on long trips.

What You Need

• *To be travelling in the car*

What To Do

As you are driving in the car, have someone point out a distant landmark or object. Everyone else guesses how far away it is.

The driver checks the kilometres on his speedo and the person with the closest estimation is the winner.

activity
229

MATCH THE TIME

8+

Children have to learn to tell the time from analogue clocks, digital clocks and written time. Games like Match the Time will help them learn this in a fun way.

What You Need

- *Analogue clock*
  (a clock or watch with a conventional round face)
- *Digital clock* • *Paper* • *Pencil*

What To Do

Show your children how time is written - 4.20 - then show them what this looks like on an analogue and a digital clock.

Draw some circles on a piece of paper and put in the hours. These will represent the analogue clocks. Next, draw some rectangles. These will represent the digital clocks.

Next, write a list of times - 4.30, 7.20, 8.48, 1.10, 8.50 and so on.

Now your children have to show these times on both the analogue and digital drawings. When they can do it with no trouble, they can set some for you to work out.

activity
230

NUMBER WORDS

8+

A fun family game to play with the children
to help improve everyone's adding-up skills.

 ✓

 ✓

What You Need

• *Paper* • *Pencils* • *Hat or box*

 ✓

What To Do

Cut up a piece of paper into 26 squares and write a letter of the alphabet on each square. Put them all into a hat or box and mix them well.

The children number their paper down the side from 1 to 26. As each letter is pulled from the hat, it is written beside the next number. Perhaps 'W' was pulled out first - if so, it will be '1'; T second - 2, M third - 3, and so on.

Now everyone makes up as many words as they can, trying to think of words with the highest possible numerical value. Set a time limit of 5 or 10 minutes, then add up everyone's scores and see who is the winner.

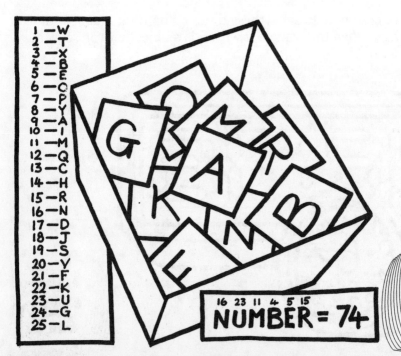

1 —W
2 —T
3 —X
4 —B
5 —E
6 —O
7 —P
8 —Y
9 —A
10 —I
11 —M
12 —Q
13 —C
14 —H
15 —R
16 —N
17 —D
18 —J
19 —S
20 —V
21 —F
22 —K
23 —U
24 —G
25 —L

16 23 11 4 5 15
NUMBER = 74

activity
231

ROUND THE CLOCK

8+

A good family game to all play together.

 ✓

 ✓

What You Need

 ✓

- *A few players*
- *Two dice*
- *Paper and pencil*

 ✓

What To Do

One player has a piece of paper and a pencil to score. Down the ✓ left-hand side write the numbers 1 to 12 below each other.
Across the top write the players' names. Draw a column for each player.

Players take it in turn to throw 1 to 12 in the correct sequence. The winner is the first to complete the sequence. The scorer ticks beside the number in each player's column as he throws the correct number.

Players throw both dice each turn. For numbers 1 to 6, a player can score with either or both dice - for instance, a 2 and a 4 could be 2, 4 or 6. It is also possible at this stage to score twice on one turn - if a player throws a 2 and a 3, he could count both numbers.

From 7 to 12, however, a player will have to add together both dice. Good counting practice!

	Timmy	Sarah	Mum	Dad
1	✓	✓	✓	✓
2	✓	✓	✓	✓
3	✓	✓		✓
4	✓	✓		
5		✓		
6		✓		
7				

activity
232

CALENDAR CALCULATIONS   10+

Help your children learn more about using calendars with these simple problems. Buy a calendar for their room so they can write in important dates.

What You Need

• *Calendar* • *Paper* • *Pencils*

What To Do

Choose the last three calendar months to work from. Set some problems for your children to solve, such as:

What date was -

The second Friday in July?
The first Thursday in June?
The last day in August?
The last Wednesday in August?

• How many days from Thursday the 14th of June until Friday the 28th of July?
• How many schooldays are there in June?
(Don't forget about public holidays and school holidays (if any).
• How many days are there from the second Saturday in June until the last Sunday in August?
• How many weeks altogether in June and July?
• How many Saturdays altogether in June, July and August?

Problems like these will help your children understand how to use a calendar and keeping one of their own will help them keep track of important events in their life.

activity
233

GALLUP POLLS

10+

Has your household ever been 'phoned to take part in an information quest - a Gallup Poll? Help your children conduct one with your own family, or perhaps among some of the kids in their class.

What You Need

• *Clipboard* • *Paper* • *Pen*

What To Do

Help your children work out the questions they will ask - if it is within the family, maybe things like bedtimes, favourite meals, favourite TV programmes, favourite holiday destinations, favourite foods - maybe vegies or even ice cream flavours. School questions might include things like favourite buses, changes to the uniform, amounts of homework, and so on.

When all the results are collected, help the children collate them. Perhaps you may have to make a few family changes!

activity
234

HOUSEHOLD PROBLEMS

10+

Help your children work out every-day mathematics problems with examples like these. Children need to realise that mathematics is needed for real life.

What You Need

• *Paper* • *Pencil* • *Your time*

What To Do

Show your child examples of the sort of problems adults solve with mathematics daily. Write some of them down and see if your children can work them out (calculators are allowed).

• Work out how much interest we will need to pay each year on a Housing Loan of $50,000 at 7.50% per annum.
• We need to paint the inside of the house. The house has 10 rooms and each room needs one tin of undercoat and one tin of top coat. The undercoat will cost $35.00 per tin and the topcoat will cost $38.00 per tin. We will also need to buy a roller for $10.00 and four new brushes at $8.00 each. How much will we be spending on paint and brushes?
• Mum is going to start going to the fruit and vegetable markets to buy cases of fruit. Each box of apples holds seven dozen apples. She wants to share the apples among five friends and her own family. Everyone wants two dozen apples. How many cases will she have to buy?
• Mum has asked you to go to the shop and buy a loaf of bread and a paper. The paper costs $0.70 and the loaf of bread is $1.85. She has given you $4.00 and said you can have the change for an iceblock. How much will you have to spend on an iceblock? Will you be able to buy your favourite, which is $1.50?

Take your children shopping with you to work out some more problems.

activity
235

MAGIC NUMBER 9

10+

Teach your children some of the 'magic' properties of number 9.

What You Need

• *Paper* • *Pencil*

What To Do

When your children are learning their nine times table, teach them some of the interesting properties of number 9.

Do they know that you can always tell whether a number is divisible by 9? Just add all the digits of the number together until you reduce it to one number. If that number is 9, the number you began with will be divisible by 9, no matter how big it is. Try 45 (4 + 5 = 9), then try 1214 (1 + 2 + 1 + 4 = 18; 1 + 8 = 9), or even 6,878,943 (6 + 8 + 7 + 8 + 9 + 4 + 3 = 45; 4 + 5 = 9). Let your children work out some of these for themselves.

Now try some number magic with the nine times table. To get the ten first results of the multiplication tables for 9, have them follow these simple steps.

Think of the number you want to multiply 9 by - say 7. Now, subtract 1 - which gives us 6. That number 6 is the first digit of your number.

Then take that number 6 from 9 and you will get the second digit of your answer - 3. The answer is 63.

(Of course, while all this is very interesting, remind your children that it will be a lot quicker to just learn their 9 times table off by heart).

activity
236

NINE MEN'S MORRIS

10+

An ancient game of skill to play with your older children.

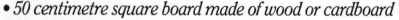

What You Need

- *50 centimetre square board made of wood or cardboard*
- *Ruler • Marking pen*
- *Counters - 9 each of a different colour, e.g. 9 reds and 9 whites*

What To Do

First, mark out the board as shown below, then give each player 9 counters of the same colour. The youngest player begins and players then take it in turns to put their counters on the board one at a time. They must be placed on one of the 24 circles forming the corners and line intersections on the board.

The players try to get three of their counters in a line (called 'a mill') while stopping their opponents doing the same thing. When a player gets three counters in a line they can take off one of their opponent's counters, but not one already forming a line of three. That counter is then out of the game.

When all the counters are on the board, the players then take it in turn to move one counter at a time along the lines to the next unoccupied point. At this stage in the game mills can be made, broken and remade. The counters must move along straight lines, however. Each time a player makes or remakes a mill, they can remove an opponent's counter.

By the end of the game, if a player has only three counters left and they are in a mill, they must break the mill on their turn. At this stage that player is no longer restricted to the paths but can 'hop' to any point on the board.

The object of the game is to capture 7 counters from the other person or create a situation where the other person cannot move.

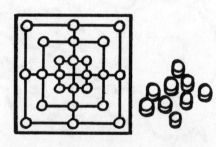

activity

237

SHOPPING CALCULATIONS   10+

A game to play with your older children to improve their calculator skills and teach them some shopping sense at the same time.

What You Need

• *Sheets of paper* • *Pencils* • *Calculators*

What To Do

Call out simple shopping equations to calculate and the children copy them down. They have to work out which items would be the cheapest - for example, 3 for $2.90 or 7 for $6.60 - or: 3 for $64.50 or 5 for $110.00.

As each equation is solved, the first person with the correct answer gets a tick or star. The person who wins the most at the end of the game gets to choose a special treat - perhaps a family picnic destination or a special dinner menu!

activity

238

SPEND THE MONEY GAME   10+

A good budgeting game to play with older children.

What You Need

• *Shop catalogues*

What To Do

Here is a quick mathematics activity that will help your children learn how to budget money.

Pretend with your children that you are going to totally make over their room.   Give them a budget - perhaps $1000 - and a few shop catalogues.

They have to buy the furniture, bedding, etc. from the catalogues and come in under the budget.

You could also play this game at Christmas time and give them a budget for the family Christmas shopping!

activity
239

SQUARE NUMBERS

10+

When your children have learnt all their multiplication tables, teach them this easy way to work out square roots of two digit numbers that end in 5.

What You Need

• *Paper* • *Pencil* • *A calculator to check the answers*

What To Do

The first step is to multiply the first digit of the number by the same digit plus one, for example 35 squared would be 3 x 4 = 12 - then simply add the number 25. The answer would be 35≤ = 1225. Have your children check with their calculator to see if you are correct.

activity
240

OUR ENVIRONMENT

AGES   **OUR ENVIRONMENT**   ACTIVITY No.

OUR ENVIRONMENT

AGES   ACTIVITY No.

BUBBLES

2+

Great fun to make on a windy day. Your children can work out which direction the wind is coming from.

What You Need

- *Detergent* • *Water* • *Container*
- *Cooking oil or glycerine*
- *Pipe cleaners or fine wire*
- *Plastic drinking straws*
- *Commercial bubble pipes*

What To Do

Make up a strong solution of bubble mixture with washing-up detergent and water. A teaspoon of cooking oil or glycerine added to the mixture makes the bubbles stronger.

Help your children make some bubble blowers out of pipe cleaners, fine wire, or just use drinking straws. Perhaps you already have some bubble blowers - large ones to make gigantic bubbles can often be bought at flea markets and provide hours of fun.

Make bubbles together and watch them float. See whose bubbles go the highest and drift the furthest. Young children love chasing the bubbles you make too!

activity
241

INSECT HUNT

2+ ✓

 ✓

Keeping insects will help your children find out more about them and foster an interest in nature.

 ✓

What You Need

- *Any small box, but a shoe box is ideal*
- *Piece of net and large rubber band or piece of elastic to hold it on*

 ✓

What To Do

Go with your children on a 'bug' hunt. Take a bottle, a fine net or a bug catcher to trap them. Make sure you collect some of the leaves you trap your bug on to put in the bug box with it.

Make sure your children understand that we only keep insects and other creatures for a short stay, after which they must be returned to their 'families'.

activity
242

MAGNET FISHING GAME

2+

A fun game to teach your children some of the properties of magnets.

What You Need

- *Piece of dowel or long stick*
- *String or thin cord*
- *Horseshoe magnet*
- *Plastic ice cream lids or styrofoam meat trays*

What To Do

Cut lots of fish or other sea creature shapes out of the ice cream lids. You could make an octopus, some sea horses, squid, sharks, starfish, and even rays, as well as fish shapes.

Place a large paper clip on the 'mouth' of each sea creature and make a fishing line by attaching the magnet with a length of cord to the pole.
You could turn a large cardboard box, or even just a pile of pillows, into a 'fishing boat'.

On hot days, take the fishing game outside and fill up the children's wading pool with water. Add a few drops of blue food colouring to the water and the kids will love fishing in the blue 'sea'.

activity
243

BALLOON MYSTERIES

4+

Do your children ask you lots of difficult-to-answer questions such as 'Why does the moon stay up in the sky?', or 'Why do balloons bounce?'
Try this simple experiment together to discover why balloons do bounce.

What You Need

• *Balloons*

What To Do

Blow up a balloon for your children and tie it so the air will not escape. Tell your children to push it down as hard as they can and bounce it against different surfaces.

What happens when they push it down hard? Explain that when you blow air into balloons the air molecules are very tightly packed together. By pushing down on the balloon you are making the molecules resist. Because the balloon and the molecules inside it are elastic, they will bounce back.

Now help your children fill a balloon with sand and another with water and see what happens. Does the balloon bounce now?

Explain that the special elastic properties of air makes it bounce, which is why tyres and sports balls are filled with air.

activity
244

FRAGRANT SHOE BOX

4+

See how well your children can distinguish different smells with this fun activity.

What You Need

- *Aromatic substances - perhaps an onion, vanilla essence, Vegemite, perfume, lemon peel, orange peel, soap, peanut paste, lavender, chocolate, etc.*
- *Shoe box*
- *Drinking straws*
- *Plastic bags*
- *Rubber bands*
- *Paper*
- *Coloured felt pens*

What To Do

Punch six holes just big enough to fit the drinking straws at intervals in the lid of the box. Put six smelling substances in plastic bags and attach the straws to the bags with rubber bands. Place them in the box and put the straws through the holes. Colour some small pieces of paper the colour of the substances, e.g. light brown for peanut paste, yellow for lemon peel, to give clues and help discussion about the scents.

Let your children smell the different scents and then talk together about what they think they are, or what they remind them of.

Happy sniffing!

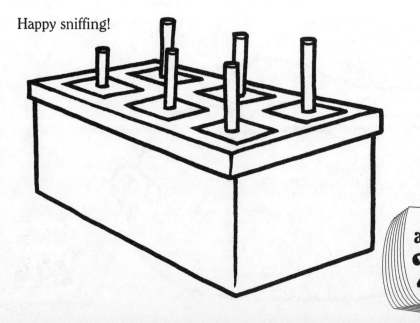

activity
245

GRASS HEADS

4+

While these can be bought from many craft markets, they are simple and fun to make with your children.

What You Need

- *Old pantihose or stockings*
- *Plastic container, e.g. margarine, yoghurt*
- *Grass seeds*
- *Potting mix*
- *Stickers or felt pens*

What To Do

Cut off one leg of the pantihose and hold it open while your children measure in at least three tablespoons of grass seeds. Then add three to four cups of potting mix. Tie the stocking securely above the potting mix and form into a round 'head', and balance in the container.

Your children will enjoy making a face on the grass head and perhaps adding a bow or bow-tie and buttons to the container.

Keep the grass head damp and in a few days it will begin to grow a head of lovely bright green hair.

activity
246

HEART BEAT

4+

Children are always fascinated by a doctor's stethoscope. Make a simple home-made version with your children and they can listen to their heart beat and play 'doctors'.

What You Need

- *2 plastic funnels*
- *1 metre of plastic tubing to fit the funnels*

What To Do

The children can help you push a funnel into each end of the plastic tubing. Push it in as hard as possible so the funnels don't come out. Place a funnel over your heart and listen to the heart beat with the other funnel over your ear. (Jumping up and down a few times increases your heart beat and makes it easier to hear.)

Explain to your children that the heart is a large pump and the stethoscope is just a device to hear it better. It works by channelling the sound waves so you can hear them more clearly.

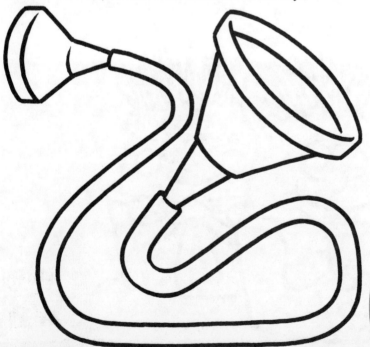

activity
247

LEAF HUNT

4+

A fun matching game to play in your own garden that will encourage your children's interest in plants and trees.

What You Need

• *Leaves from plants in your garden.*

What To Do

Collect a variety of leaves from different plants in the garden and show them to your children.

Then go for a walk around the garden with your children and see if they can match the leaves to the plant they come from. (If you don't have a garden, do it in a local park).

(Later your children can try leaf rubbings. Place the leaf with the vein side up on a piece of paper. Put a piece of paper over the leaf and holding it very still, rub over the pages with the side of a pencil or crayon. You will see the shape emerge and all the veins and stem clearly on the rubbing).

Leaf

activity
248

MAGNET FUN

4+

Young children enjoy using magnets and finding out how they work. Explain to your children that magnets were made from a special sort of rock named magnetite or lodestone and they attract iron and steel. Show them that magnets have two poles, a north and a south, and how magnets can repel and attract each other. Buy a pair of similar strength magnets so your children will have the opportunity to discover the qualities of magnets for themselves.

What You Need

• *Collection of small items made from different materials, such as coins, safety pins, hair clips, small toys, stones, sticks, nails, buttons, pegs, cutlery*

What To Do

Let your children try each item with the magnet to see which ones are attracted by the magnet and which are not.

Try to help your children understand the concept of objects being pulled or attracted to the magnet rather than 'stick' like glue sticks.

Go around the house finding which other items and appliances are 'magnetic'.

Later they might enjoy a magnet 'treasure hunt'. Hide some small metal items in a dish of sand and they can use their magnet to hunt for the 'treasures' in the sand.

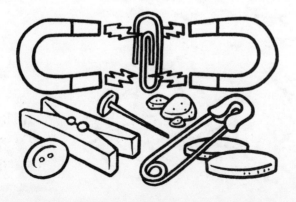

activity
249

MOBILE PHONES!

4+

Make a simple 'phone' with your children and whisper secrets.

What You Need

• *Two funnels*
• *Length of plastic tubing that fits the funnel ends*

What To Do

Connect this simple 'phone' by pushing the funnel ends into the tubing.   If you buy a really big length you can be in different rooms and still tell secrets.

Your children will love being able to talk to each other from different rooms - somehow they fight less that way!

If you don't have funnels, tins work well also connected to the tubing or just to string.

When they lose interest in the phones, put the tubing into shorter lengths and they'll have lots of fun in the bath with the funnels and tubing.

activity
250

NEIGHBOURHOOD PLAY MAT 4+

Make a play mat of your own neighbourhood for your children to use with their little cars and trucks. A great way to teach simple mapping skills to young children.

What You Need

- *A sheet of heavy duty white vinyl*
- *Permanent marking pens in a variety of colours*

What To Do

Discuss with your children the features of your neighbourhood - where the roads go, the houses, parks, local shops and any other familiar landmarks. Then carefully mark them on the vinyl (you might like to do it in pencil or coloured chalk first and then draw over in permanent pen when you are happy with the result.)

Mark your home, your neighbours' homes, the local streets, the school, the parks, shops and anything else your children are familiar with. Go for walks together and talk about the landmarks you could put on their map. When it is made, they will have great fun playing with it and learning about how maps are made as they play.

activity

251

PLANT A TREE

4+

Help your children develop a love of gardening and care for the environment with this long term project.

What You Need

- *A small tree to plant*
- *Gardening books or magazines*
- *Your camera*
- *A notebook for a tree diary*

What To Do

Planting a tree on Arbor Day in spring was a tradition in Queensland schools when I was growing up. Revive this old idea with your children in your own garden.

Look through gardening magazines and books (borrow some from your local library if you do not have them at home) to find a tree suitable for your local climate and for the size of your garden.

Take your children to the nursery with you. Help them plant the tree at home and make them responsible for its care.

Don't forget to take photos of them planting and caring for their tree and yearly photos to add to their diary, recording both their growth.

Also for their diary, they could -

Do rubbings of the tree's bark
Press the flowers
Learn to use a tape measure to measure its height and girth
Do leaf rubbings of the leaves.

If you don't have room to plant a tree, your children could 'adopt' a tree in a local park and do the same activities there.

activity
252

PULSE BEAT

4+ ✓

 ✓

Show your children a simple way of finding out if their heart is beating with this easy experiment.

 ✓

What You Need

• *Toothpicks* • *Playdough or plasticine*

What To Do

Form a small ball of playdough and stick a toothpick into it. Have your children hold out their arm straight and keep it totally still. Place the ball of playdough on their wrist where the pulse is. (You may need to move it around to find the strongest beat). Watch what happens to the toothpick.

Have your children run around for a little while or jump up and down a few times, and let them observe their pulse after exercise. Put the playdough ball on your own arm and they can see your pulse also.

Explain to your children that they saw the toothpick move because they are seeing the blood flow through their blood vessels to their heart. Doctors measure pulse rates to find out if a person's heart is beating at a normal rate.

They might enjoy counting the pulse rates of various members of the family and see who has the fastest heart beat.

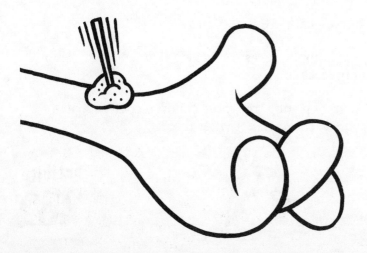

activity
253

RIVERS IN THE SANDPIT

4+

On hot days the hose in the sandpit is most children's idea of heaven. Turn a blind eye to the mess and the wet clothes and help turn it into a great geography lesson.

What You Need

• *The sandpit* • *Hose*

What To Do

Join your children in the sandpit and bring the hose. Suggest you could make a little creek together. Dig out the creek and let the hose run into it - soon there will be billabongs, waterfalls, lakes and, eventually, a big river. Explain and name these features and compare them to real ones you have seen together. When it becomes too wet, turn off the hose, have a morning tea picnic, and then watch as the 'drought' dries up all the water.

Next time you go for a drive in the country together, look for the geographical features in real life that you made together in the sandpit.

activity
254

SNAIL MYSTERIES

4+

Do you have lots of snails in your garden? Children are fascinated by snails and they will love finding out how old the snails are.

What You Need

• *Snails*
• *A magnifying glass (most newsagents sell these)*

What To Do

Carefully look at the snails under the magnifying glass. Can you see the rings on their shells? Count the rings on each snail's shell and see which has the most. That snail is the oldest.

Explain to your children that, as the snail grows inside its shell, the shell must grow from the edge and so more and more rings are added. Each ring means a growth spurt.

Trees have rings too. Next time you see a log, see if you can count the growth rings and see how old the tree was.

activity
255

SPRING FLOWER PICTURES   4+

A beautiful way to preserve some of the spring flowers from your garden.

What You Need

- *Small flowers and leaves* • *Iron*
- *Waxed or grease proof paper*

What To Do

Go for a walk in your garden with your children and pick some flowers and leaves to make spring flower pictures. Small flat flowers work best for this project.

On a piece of waxed paper help your children arrange the flowers as artistically as they can. Then place another sheet of waxed paper on the top and iron carefully with a cool iron. The wax in the paper will bind together and seal the flowers inside.

Draw around the outside of the flowers with a thick marking pen - perhaps a heart or flower shape and your children can cut it out.

They look great Blu-Tacked on windows or use to decorate the front of their own gift cards.

activity
256

SPROUTING SEEDS

4+

Your children can help add some variety to the family salads and sandwiches by growing their own sprouts.

What You Need

- *Seeds - such as mung beans, alfalfa, lentils, soy beans (best bought from a Health Food Shop so you know they are free from chemicals).*
- *Strainer or colander* • *Large glass jar*
- *Piece of thin cloth such as muslin, cheese cloth or net*

What To Do

Help your children measure half a cup of seeds into a strainer. (For larger seeds use a colander). Rinse well under running water. Pick out any damaged seeds and then place in the large jar. Pour in three cups of tepid water and leave to soak overnight. Next morning rinse again in the strainer then return the seeds to the jar and cover with the fine cloth. Secure around the top with a strong rubber band or piece of elastic. At least three times a day rinse the seeds well by filling the jar with tap water and draining through the cloth. Keep the seeds in a cool dark place - the kitchen pantry is ideal.

In a few days the seeds will be ready to eat and you and your children can concoct some yummy salads for the family.

activity
257

TEXTURE RUBBINGS

4+ ✓

Develop your children's interest in their environment by showing them how to do texture rubbings.

 ✓

 ✓

What You Need

 ✓

- *Paper* • *Crayons or pencils*
- *Textures around your house and garden*

What To Do

 ✓

Go on a 'texture hunt' together. Place the paper over car tyres, bark, leaves, carpet, coins, tiles, flowers, bricks and any other interesting textures you can think of. Your children then rub with their crayons or pencils. Label the textures rubbings for them so they can show them to the rest of the family.

Later you may like to play 'mystery rubbings' together. Rub some new things and then they go on a 'mystery rubbings' hunt to track them down and do matching rubbings.

activity
258

TORCH GAMES

4+

A torch makes a great gift for young children. Having their own torch close at hand can make them more secure in a dark bedroom.

What You Need

• *A torch*

What To Do

Your children can help you go on a 'treasure hunt' to collect lots of items made of different materials. Collect some made of wood, plastic, paper, metal, china and fabric.

Go outside when it's really dark, or turn off all the lights and darken a room completely.

Your children then turn on their torches and work out which objects are shiny and which are dull. They will enjoy finding out which objects the torch light will shine through and which are opaque.

Torches are great for shadow games also. Perhaps one warm night you could go for a walk together and look for 'spooky' shapes and then find out what they really are!

activity
259

WINDMILLS

4+ ✓

 ✓

 ✓

 ✓

 ✓

On a windy day coloured windmills are lots of fun to make and watch spin in the wind.

What You Need

- *Paper* • *Pins*
- *Drinking straws or small sticks*

What To Do

Draw up some squares on some coloured paper for the children to cut out. Talk about what makes a square different from a rectangle while they are cutting. Next, help them draw four lines with a ruler from each corner to near the middle of each square (see the illustration below).

Bring the outside of each triangle into the middle and secure with a pin or drawing pin poked into the drinking straw.

Take them outside and hold them in the wind and watch how fast they fly.

activity
260

ANT FARMS

6+

Children are fascinated by small creatures like ants and spiders. Help your children learn more about ants by building an Ant Farm together.

What You Need

- *Large plastic soft drink bottle*
- *Drinking glass*
- *Garden soil*

What To Do

Cut the soft drink bottle in half with a Stanley or sharp knife. Discard the top section. Find a drinking glass that will fit inside, leaving a space about 4 cm wide between the glass and the plastic bottle (it should not be any wider or you will not be able to see the ants and their tunnels).

Carefully spoon in garden soil to fill the spaces. Add some ants from the garden and cover the top with some flyscreen so they cannot escape. Add a very small amount of cake, sugar or honey-soaked bread every few days.

Your children will be enthralled by the ants' busy lives and by their tunneling skills.

Although you may consider ants in the garden to be pests (we do when they dig up the sand between the pavers!), it is best to teach your children to have respect for animal life by returning the ants to their natural habitat after a few days.

activity
261

COLD FLIES

6+ ✓

 ✓

Help your children learn more about living things with this simple science experiment.

 ✓

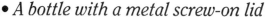

What You Need

• *A bottle with a metal screw-on lid*
• *A hammer and nail* • *Flies*

 ✓

What To Do

 ✓

Punch some holes in the lid with the hammer. Catch a fly to put in the bottle and replace the lid.

Next, put the bottle in the refrigerator for a few minutes, then take it out and together see what has happened to the flies. Explain to your children that the cold has slowed down the fly's metabolism (the energy producing process of living things) so the fly cannot move as quickly as before.

Discuss together or read books about animals that hibernate in cold weather. When the flies have warmed up, watch them return to normal and then let them go.

activity
262

FINGERPRINTS

6+

Explain to your children that everyone has different fingerprints. They can then fingerprint the whole family!

What You Need

- *Stamp pad* • *Cornflour*
- *Small soft paintbrush* • *Magnifying glass*

What To Do

Help your children fingerprint all the family by putting their index finger on the stamp pad and rolling it backwards and forwards. Then place the finger on a piece of paper and again roll it backwards and forwards. Help them write the person's name beside each fingerprint.

Now they can play the detective and look for fingerprints in the house and see if they can identify them. When they find one, show them how to lightly dust it with cornflour using a little paintbrush. Then they carefully blow away the excess cornflour and they'll be able to clearly see the fingerprint. They may need to use a magnifying glass to clearly identify the print. Sherlock Holmes!

Now you'll be able to find out who's been raiding the 'fridge and bikkie jar!

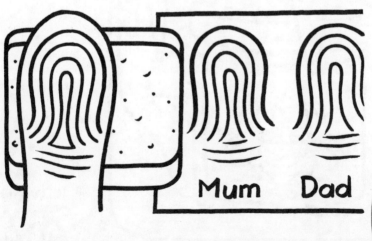

Mum   Dad

activity
263

FRUIT STICKERS

6+

Children love to collect things, and collecting fruit stickers is a fun cheap way to begin being a 'collector'! Your children will gain valuable mathematics concepts in a fun way as they sort, classify and order their fruit stickers.

What You Need

• *Scrap book* • *Stickers from fruit*

What To Do

Most fruit today comes with small stickers on it telling us the variety and sometimes where it comes from. Help your children save the stickers from their apples (or bananas, oranges, mandarins and other fruit).

They can stick them in a scrap book under the various varieties of fruit, thus learning to sort and classify, eg.

Apples - Delicious
   Granny Smith
   Golden Delicious
   Hi Early
   Jonathans

If they are marked where they come from, help them trace a large map of Australia for the front of their scrapbook and they can put some of the stickers on the places they are grown. A great geography lesson and also a healthy eating activity - make it a rule they can only have the stickers off fruit they eat!

activity
264

LAVENDER SACHETS

6+

Most Australian gardens have a bush of one of the many lovely lavender varieties. When your lavender is flowering profusely, pick the flowers to make delightful scented lavender sachets together.

What You Need

- *Lavender flowers*
- *Muslin or other thin cloth*
- *Narrow lavender ribbon*
- *Large bottle*
- *Marking pen*
- *Pinking shears*

What To Do

Together, pick flower heads that are nearly all open and spread them in the sun for a few days to dry. The flowers are easily detached by running your fingers along the stem to strip off the dried flowers.

Make the muslin sachets by tracing around a bottle with chalk and then cutting out the circles with pinking shears. Your children can put a few spoonfuls of the lavender flowers in the middle of each muslin circle and then tie securely with the lavender ribbon.

Put some lavender sachets on coathangers in your wardrobes, in drawers with clothes and in the linen cupboard. The crisp, strong smell helps repel insects.

They also make great gifts.

activity
265

LET'S FIND OUT

6+

Help your children develop their inquiring minds by posing these questions about the insects they find in the garden.

What You Need

- *Insects*
- *See 'Insect Hunt'- activity **242***

What To Do

After you have gone on an 'Insect Hunt' with your children and they have caught something to investigate, pose some of these questions.

What does it eat? - leaves, other insects, grains, nectar, wood or sap?

What does it look like? - Is it multi or one colour?
Is it dull or shiny?
Can it be camouflaged?

Where does it live? - In flowers, on leaves or stems, in plants or water?

How does it move? - Does it fly, crawl, burrow?
Does it fly quickly, slowly, straight or in zig zags?

Does it have - Wings and how many?
Legs and how many?
Feelers and how many?

What happens if you go near it or even touch it?

Older children may like to start a 'bug book'. Photograph or help your children draw the insect, see if you can identify it and then list all the characteristics you have discovered.

Have your children show their teacher at school.

All this may lead on to an interesting project for the whole class.

activity

266

LOOKING FOR RAINBOWS 6+

Children love looking at rainbows. With a few basic things, you can delight them by showing them how to make their own.

What You Need

- *A prism (chandeliers have prisms)* • *Torch*
- *Bubble water and a bubble pipe or wand* • *Mirror*
- *Shallow plastic tray* • *White paper* • *Machine oil*

What To Do

Look through a prism together to see a beautiful rainbow. Blow some bubbles in the sunlight and look for the rainbows. Take a bowl of water out into the sunlight, drop in a few drops of machine oil and, hey presto! Rainbows!

Another rainbow maker is to put a mirror in a bowl of water in the sunlight and look for the rainbows there, or shine a torch on the mirror while your children hold a piece of paper to catch the rainbow.

Don't forget to tell them the old tale of the pot of gold at the end of the rainbow and talk about the colours that make up the rainbow - they may not know colours such as indigo or violet.

Then provide some new paints or felt pens so they can create their own colourful rainbow pictures.

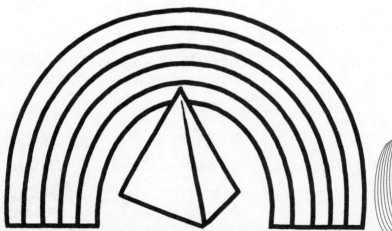

activity
267

MOONLIGHT HIKE

6+

Take your family with you on a moonlight hike.

What You Need
- *Torch*
- *Clear moonlit night*

What To Do

Put on your joggers and go for a moonlight walk in a nature reserve.   You could all listen to the sounds of the night and try to identify noises you wouldn't hear in the day.

Stay very still and you might see some nocturnal animals, such as fruit bats, possums, or even wombats.

Together look at the shapes and colours of the night; observe how different the sky appears, look at flowers and trees, and look at the shapes of houses, cars and each other.

When you come home, read some books from the library about nocturnal creatures.   Did you see any of them?

activity
268

NIGHT SKIES

6+

Spend some time at night looking at the sky with your children and help them understand more about the universe.

What You Need

• *Clear warm nights*

What To Do

Go outside with your children at night in summer and observe the sky together.   Over a period of weeks, watch the changes in the moon.   Look at the stars and, using a star guide, see if you can find some star patterns (the easiest, of course, is the Southern Cross).

See what other things you can observe at night - shooting stars, fruit bats, birds, clouds and planes.

Borrow some books from your local library and help your children learn more about our galaxy.   Toy shops and newsagents sell luminous stars and moons.   Make a 'night sky' on the ceiling of your children's room.

activity
269

ONION POWER

6+

 ✓

 ✓

My children are always amused when Mummy cries when chopping up onions. They are not so amused when I put one near them! Ask your children to chop up an onion and explain what is happening to their eyes.

 ✓

 ✓

 ✓

What You Need

• *An onion* • *Chopping board* • *Knife*

What To Do

When your children peel the onion and chop it, their eyes will begin to water. Why is it so?

Explain that onions contain a highly irritating oil that combines with the air when we are chopping them. This becomes a vapour that affects nerve glands that are actually in our noses, but connect to our eyes. This is how a strong smell or even a sneeze can make our eyes water.

Try some ways with your children to see if you can stop onions making eyes water. Some people say to keep them in the refrigerator, or peel them under running water, or even peel them with sunglasses on! See what other creative solutions your children can come up with.

Other substances can have the same effect - try (carefully) with some spices and chilli.

activity
270

OVAL EGGS

6+

Have your children ever wondered why eggs aren't round? This is one of the eternal questions children ask poor parents. Try this simple experiment together to discover why.

What You Need

- *A hard-boiled egg*
- *A tennis ball or other small round ball*

What To Do

Put both the egg and the ball on the floor and roll them. Which is easier to roll? Can your children work out why?

Explain to them that if eggs were round they would roll so easily they could roll out of the nest. The oval shape is also stronger and less likely to break.

activity

271

ROCKETS

6+

Help your children understand about propulsion and what happens to air under pressure with this interesting experiment.

What You Need

- *2 chairs* • *Drinking straw* • *Masking tape*
- *Pieces of string about 2 to 2.5 metres long*
- *Balloon (as large and as long as you can find)*

What To Do

Thread the string through the straw and tie the chairs together about two metres apart. Move the chairs apart until the string is stretched tight. Next, blow up the balloon and hold it firmly tight as you tape it to the straw. Then release the balloon! Your children will be fascinated by the result.

Explain that when you blew up the balloon, the air molecules were forced into it and, although we could not see them, they were tightly packed. When the balloon was released, the air escaped with so much force that the balloon was propelled along the string.

Explain that rockets use similar force, but not with air. Rockets use rocket fuel. Sky rockets that we see at fireworks displays use gunpowder as force, as do firearms.

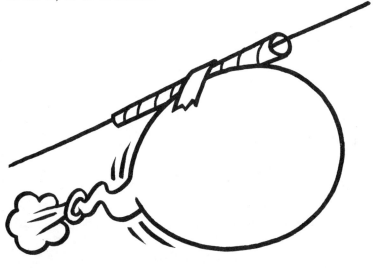

activity
272

SILK WORMS

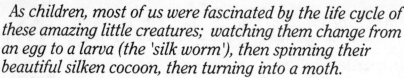

6+

As children, most of us were fascinated by the life cycle of these amazing little creatures; watching them change from an egg to a larva (the 'silk worm'), then spinning their beautiful silken cocoon, then turning into a moth.

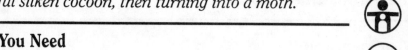

What You Need

- *Silk worms (try your local pet shop, look for ads in the paper, or ask at your local primary school. They are available around August or September)*
- *A shoe box*   • *Mulberry leaves*

What To Do

If you are lucky enough to be given eggs, your children can watch the change in the eggs. Mostly, however, you will be given the small silkworms. As they grow the silkworms increase their weight thousands of times. Older children will be able to measure and weigh (use a very tiny set of kitchen scales) and graph the results.

Isolate one silkworm and keep a count of how many mulberry leaves it can eat in a day. Older children will also be able to record changes weekly. Your children will be able to observe the caterpillars moulting also - when the silkworms become very inactive as their skin is stretched and while they are getting ready to shed it. Look at the changes in the new skin - it will be darker and wrinkly to allow room for more growth.

The next most fascinating stage is when the silkworms begin to spin their cocoons. Explain to your children that at this stage it is no longer a silkworm, but a pupa. The cocoons must not be bumped or handled, but just watched for the next three weeks.

Finally, the adult moth will emerge from the hard cocoon but, in doing so, it destroys the cocoon. Use some of the cocoons for spinning (see Silkworms - Spinning the Cocoon, activity **274**), but keep the rest so you will have a supply of eggs for next year's silk worms.

Put all the moths in a clean, dry shoe box in a cool place. Now the moths will mate and lay eggs. The male moth then dies and the female does also after laying approximately 500 eggs. Keep the eggs in a cool cupboard until next year, when the cycle will begin again.

Some other activities to try together:
- take photos of the stages
- your children can draw pictures of each stage - older children can write the story also
- do rubbings of the mulberry leaves
- look for other sorts of caterpillars to keep and observe.

activity
273

SILK WORMS - SPINNING THE COCOON 6+
(see Silk Worms - activity 273)

As well as watching the life cycle of the silk worm, your children will enjoy spinning the silk from some of the cocoons. Make a simple spinner with directions below.

What You Need • *Lead pencil* • *Old cotton reel* • *Drinking glass* • *Wood glue*

What To Do

When I was a child my father made me a silk spinner from four pieces of dowel, but this simpler version works just as well.

Push the pencil through the hole in the cotton reel and glue in place.

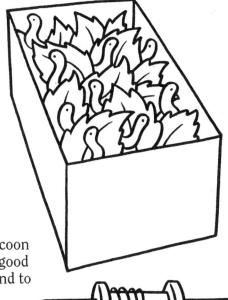

Put the cocoon into a glass that is half filled wwth warm water. You'll then be able to easily peel off the loose outside layer of the cocoon. Next, find the end of the thread and wind it around the cotton reel. Put the cocoon back in the glass and begin winding.

Keep some of the silk on each cocoon to protect the eggs, but it's also a good idea to keep a few cocoons unwound to be sure to hatch out some moths.

Take the silk off carefully and tie together
to form a narrow piece about 30 cm long. It makes a great book mark.

Show your children some real silk - perhaps look in a haberdashery for some silk fabrics.

Go to the library together to find some books about the silk industry in China. You'll all learn something new!

activity
274

SKIN DEEP

6+

As we age, our skin loses its elasticity and becomes older and lined. With a magnifying glass your children will enjoy seeing the differences in skin as it ages.

What You Need

- *A magnifying glass*
- *Children and adults of different ages*

What To Do

Take a magnifying glass along to a family gathering and your children will be astonished by the differences between older and younger hands.

Explain to them that skin is actually an organ of the body and expands and contracts as you grow and lose weight.   Unfortunately, as we age, our skin becomes less elastic and will not so easily contract to its original shape.   Let them examine their own hands, then yours, then Grandma's and Grandpa's.   Apply some hand lotion to your hands and let them see if this makes any difference.

Don't forget to remind them that the sun can damage skin and, to keep it looking young longer, they must always remember to SLIP SLOP SLAP!

activity
275

SOLAR SYSTEM MOBILE

6+

When your children really become fascinated by outer space and our solar system, help them make a solar system mobile to hang above their bed.

What You Need

- *An old umbrella* • *Yellow paint* • *Fishing line*
- *Cardboard* • *Silver spray paint or alfoil*
- *Polystyrene balls*
  (available in different sizes from craft shops)

What To Do

Together, remove all the fabric from an old umbrella, then make the 'solar system'. Paint the largest polystyrene ball yellow and cover the others with silver alfoil or spray paint silver. Cut some cardboard stars and moons.

Borrow some books about space from your local library to get the exact positioning of all the planets, then attach them all with fishing line to the umbrella.

Buy a pack of 'glow in the dark' stars from a toyshop and stick these to the ceiling, too. Your children will want to spend a lot of time lying on their bed!

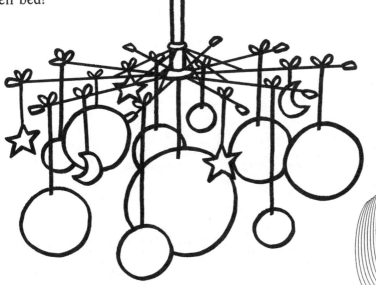

activity
276

SPIDERS

Help your child learn more about spiders and their importance in our environment.

What You Need

• *A spider and its web to observe*

What To Do

Find a spider's web in the garden and watch it together for a few days. See what the spider does in the daytime and come out with a torch at night and observe its activity. Watch the small insects it has caught in the web and see how long the spider takes to eat them.

If you can find an old uninhabited web, you can make a 'Web Picture' by lightly spraying the spider's web with white spray paint. Hold a piece of black paper behind the web and at the anchoring points of the web. The wet paint will stick the web onto the paper. Your children will be amazed by the spider's line work.

It's fun to go into the garden early in the morning also and watch any spider's web glistening with dew. Look at the shapes in the web and see how many squares, triangles, rectangles and even hexagons and pentagons you can find.

Talk about safety and spiders also. See if you can find a book at the library about spiders and read it together.

activity
277

TERRARIUM GARDEN

6+

A simple and inexpensive way to make a little garden with your children - ideal for unit dwellers.

What You Need

- *Large plastic soft drink bottle with a black base*
- *Potting mix* • *Small plants or seeds*

What To Do

Cut the soft drink bottle in half with a stanley knife and then soak the bottom half in warm water until the clear plastic comes out of the black base. When this section is inverted and pushed into the black base, you have a simple but most effective terrarium to make a little garden in, with your children.

Fill the base with some good quality potting mix and plant together with small plants or seeds. Water it and then seal. Terrariums are best kept in a warm spot away from direct sunlight. They will only need watering every ten days as it is a sealed environment like a hot house, so be careful not to over water.

Terrariums make ideal places to raise seeds in cooler climates, and to grow cuttings. Happy gardening!

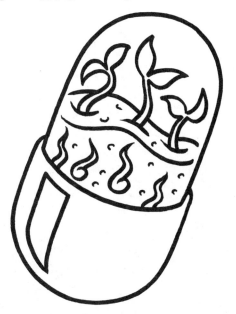

activity
278

USING THE STREET DIRECTORY   6+

Use your local street directory to help your children learn about maps.

What You Need

• *Street directory or map of your local area*

What To Do

Before you go for walks with your children, or short drives in the car together, look up where you are going in your street directory. Work out a route together and take it with you. Check it as you turn corners and change directions. Look for local landmarks such as schools, churches, shopping centres and parks on the map.

As your children gain mapping skills, make them the 'navigator' for longer trips to places you have not been before. Keep your cool! You will probably get lost a few times, but many adults go through their whole lives without ever developing a good sense of direction. Help your children gain mastery over this important life skill in a fun and relaxing way. Besides, all the walks will be great for your own fitness level!

activity
279

WIND CHIMES

6+

Make some simple wind-chimes with your children and you will all take delight in their pretty tinkly sounds on windy days.

What You Need

- *Wind-chimes can be made from many different materials such as: Clay, bamboo, shells, horseshoes, seedpods, pieces of wood, bells, etc.*
- *Fishing line or thin string*   • *Branches of wood*

What To Do

Decide together what you are going to make some wind-chimes from. You will need to help with drilling holes or tying knots.

When they are finished, hang them from a convenient tree branch and enjoy the music of the wind.

activity
280

WORM HOUSE

It's easy to find a worm to have to stay for a while and watch. Make a simple Worm House with your children so they can learn more about these small animals.

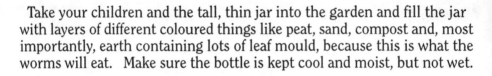

What You Need

- *Worms* • *Tall, thin jar*
- *Sand, earth, peat moss or compost*

What To Do

Take your children and the tall, thin jar into the garden and fill the jar with layers of different coloured things like peat, sand, compost and, most importantly, earth containing lots of leaf mould, because this is what the worms will eat. Make sure the bottle is kept cool and moist, but not wet.

Dig in the garden together until you find a worm. Put it on the top of the bottle so your children have a good chance to observe it.

As the worm tunnels down through the layers it feeds on the earth, and what it exudes is called the worm-cast. Your children will be able to watch the patterns the worm makes as it moves through the layers of dirt.

When your children have learnt all they can about worms, make sure you dig a hole together and place the worm back in the garden.

Find out more about worms from your local library or even invest in a Worm Farm to make great compost for the garden.

activity

281

CRYSTAL MAKING

8+

Help your children understand more about how rocks are formed by making some easy crystals from sugar.

What You Need

- *2 cups of sugar*
- *1 cup of boiling water*
- *Food colouring*
- *Shallow bowl*
- *Wooden kebab sticks or pieces of string*

What To Do

Carefully stir the sugar into the boiling water, add a few drops of food colouring and let it cool to room temperature.

Your children will enjoy arranging the kebab sticks or pieces of string in the bowl. Then they slowly and carefully pour on the sugar solution. Cover and let it stand for a few days. More and more crystals will form as the mixture stands.

Instead of adding the food colouring at the start, your children could add drops of different food colouring with an eye dropper to the crystals to make a garden-like effect.

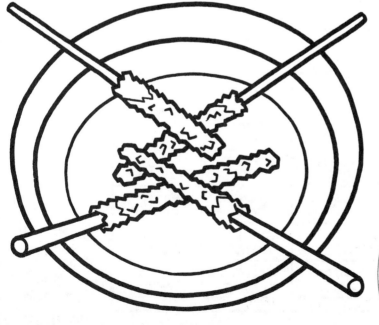

activity
282

GENE POWER

8+

Genetics are big news in today's world, with new genetic breakthroughs being discovered almost daily. Help your children understand what genes are and how they affect us all.

What You Need

• *Pencil* • *Paper*

What To Do

Help your children list all the members of your immediate family on the top of a large piece of paper. Under each family member help them think of physical characteristics of that person - their eye colour, hair colour, hair type (curly, wavy or straight), ear shape (detached or undetached lobes), and perhaps even whether they can curl their tongue.

Remind your children that all of these characteristics are inherited and that we have dominant and recessive genes. Work out how individual family members are similar and yet different.

Remind your children that Genetics is the science of why living things behave and look the way they do. Inside each cell are tiny chromosomes which carry different genetic messages and help make us what we are. Explain to your children that they receive a mixture of genes from both parents and they can see sometimes which parent provided which characteristic. 'Thanks, Dad, for the big nose!'

Mum	Dad	Timmy	Sarah
brown hair	red hair	brown hair	red hair
blue eyes	brown eyes	brown eyes	blue eyes
wavy hair	straight hair	straight hair	wavy hair
small nose	big nose	small nose	small nose
mole on neck	scar on cheek	birthmark on arm	scar on knee

activity

283

NATURE SCAVENGER HUNT

8+

*A good game to play in the backyard,
at the beach or in a park.*

What You Need

- *Paper* • *Pencils*
- *Paper or plastic bags*

What To Do

Make a list of 10 to 20 things you may be able to find in a
particular area. Protect the environment by making sure living plants or
animals are not on the list. You will have to check out the area first to
see just what sort of things you can put on the list.

At the beach you could list items such as a broken shell, a perfect shell,
a stone, some seaweed, driftwood and so on. In a park the list could
include a pine cone, a gumnut, a white stone, a brown leaf, etc.

Each child has a copy of the list and a bag for the 'treasures'. Set a time
limit and, at the end, the person who has found the most items is the
winner.

activity
284

POT POURRI

8+

Help your children store the flower scents of spring and summer blossoms by turning them into beautiful, fragrant pot pourri.

What You Need

- *Lots of scented flowers - roses, carnations, annuals, freesias, lavender and so on*
- *Orris powder (available from chemists)*
- *Mixed spice or allspice*   • *Brown sugar*
- *Large storage bottle with a lid*   • *Salt*

What To Do

Early one warm morning, gather all the flowers you will need together (at least enough for about three cupfuls of petals). Stand the flowers in a bucket of water for a day. Then the children will love stripping off all the petals. Put them in a shady place on newspaper for a few days and turn them at least once a day. When the petals are dry and stiff, you can make the pot pourri.

Mix together: 1 tablespoon orris powder
              5 tablespoons of spices
              1 tablespoon of sugar

Put a layer of petals in a large jar and sprinkle on lots of salt.   Then sprinkle over a small handful of spices. Do this in layers until the petals are all used up.

Stir every couple of days for about three weeks. By then the oils and scents will have mingled. Pot Pourri is great in bowls in the house as room fresheners, or your children might like to give it away for gifts. When it begins to lose its fragrance, add a few drops of an essential oil like Boronia or Lavender to refresh it.

activity
285

PRESSED FLOWER CARDS

8+

Preserve the beauty of your garden by making pressed flower cards with your children. A special gift to give to grandparents, other relatives and friends.

What You Need

- *Flowers* • *Telephone books*
- *Absorbent paper - kitchen paper or blotting paper*
- *Cardboard*

What To Do

Gather small flowers from the garden - preferably using ones the size of a five cent or ten cent piece. Some flowers press better than others, so you will have to experiment together.

There are many flower presses on the market and if your children really become interested in this hobby, one of them would make a lovely gift. However, old telephone books work just as well. Press the flowers between the kitchen paper and help the children place them between the pages. Leave at least 20 pages between each set of flowers. Stack some heavy books or even bricks on top of the telephone books and leave for a couple of weeks.

Help your children cut out the card, draw oval or round shapes on the front and creatively arrange the pressed flowers, glueing in place with dots of craft glue. Leaves, a little lace and ribbon and some grasses can all be glued with the flowers for a pretty effect.

Perhaps you could frame one of their creations to hang also!

activity
286

SHELL MOBILE

8+

Keep holiday memories alive by collecting shells and driftwood at the beach and make a shell mobile together.

What You Need

- *Pieces of driftwood*
- *Shells with small holes in them* • *Fishing line*

What To Do

Next time you are at the beach, collect as many shells as you can find that have small holes in them. These are quite easy to find. Also see if you can find some interesting pieces of driftwood.

When you come home help your children thread the shells with the fishing lines. (You won't be able to use a bodkin or tapestry needle as the holes in shells are usually too tiny).

Attach the threading to the driftwood and hang outside in the breeze.

The delightful tinkling will bring back lots of holiday memories.

activity
287

SNAILS

8+ ✓

Help your children learn more about these fascinating creatures.

 ✓

What You Need

- *Snails from the garden*
- *Aquarium or very large glass jar*

 ✓

What To Do

 ✓

When snails invade your garden, before you reach for the snail bait, collect a few for your children to observe and study for a few days. It's fun to go on a snail hunt together at night with a torch - you'll find lots more that way.

Put the snails you have collected in the aquarium and give them some food - lettuce is ideal, in fact that is what they are given to cleanse them before eating.

Your children will enjoy seeing the snail's large foot as it travels across the glass using its wave-like contractions. Observe the mucous trail that is left, which protects the snail from sharp surfaces. Did you know snails can crawl over very sharp objects without being hurt? Put a razor blade or sharp knife in the aquarium and watch.

Snail races are fun too! Mark the snails with different coloured stickers on their shells and put them on a marked path. Time the snails to see how far they can move in a minute.

Your children will be fascinated to learn that snails are considered to be gourmet fare in France and Japan. If they are adventurous eaters, buy a jar of snails from a good deli and cook them gently in butter and garlic. Yummy!

Make your children's snails the focus of a school project or talk to the class. Go to the local library together and find out more interesting facts about snails. Their classmates and teachers will be fascinated too!

activity

288

WATTLE SEED OLYMPICS

8+

This game will help your children gain an understanding of how plants survive and reproduce.

What You Need

• *Wattle seed pods.*

What To Do

After your wattle trees have flowered in winter they produce seed pods. Most of these seed pods are aerodynamically designed to spread in the wind over a very wide area.

Collect lots of seed pods with your children and take them up on a verandah (always watch young children carefully in high places).

Let the seed pods go and watch carefully to see which go the furthest, which take the longest and shortest time to hit the ground, which twist the most, and perhaps which hit a certain target you have marked earlier.

If you are doing this on a windy day the seed pods will get blown further and your children will have the opportunity to see how wind helps spread seeds.

When you go for walks, or to parks with your children, take a bag to collect other interesting 'flying' seeds.

activity
289

SOLAR POWER

10+

Kids today are really environmentally conscious and are truly concerned about saving fossil fuel and conserving our natural resources. Try this simple experiment to find out which materials absorb heat best and see if you can make some changes with your kids to the way your household uses heating fuels.

What You Need

- *Pencil and paper*
- *A variety of objects such as a dark house-brick, white vinyl, curtain lining, carpet square, a ceramic tile, some alfoil and white paper*

What To Do

This activity is best done on a hot, sunny day. Put all the objects chosen for the experiment out in the full sun. Come back in a couple of hours and see which objects are the hottest and which are the coolest. The children can order the heat-absorbing properties of each material from the most effective to the least effective.

Talk together about ideas they have to make your home cooler in summer and warmer in winter. Go for a walk together and see how many houses in your area have solar heaters on their roof. You may even see some homes with solar heating for swimming pools on their roofs. Think of ways your family can save power - always wash clothes on sunny days so you don't use the clothes dryer, or have a lap rug each in winter instead of using the heater; or turn off your electric blanket when you get into bed instead of leaving it on all night!

activity
290

TAKE IT APART

10+

Develop your children's interest in how things work by letting them take things apart.

What You Need

• *Screwdriver* • *A pair of pliers* • *Old appliances*

What To Do

If your kids are interested in how things work (and there are very few who aren't!), develop their inquiring minds by letting them take apart simple broken appliances instead of just throwing them out.

Always keep safety a high priority. Cut off any power cords first and, of course, appliances that must remain sealed such as TV's, refrigerators, microwaves and freezers are not to be touched.

However, items such as bike parts, broken toys, clocks, watches, phones, old radios (not with tubes), small appliances such as toasters and hairdryers, torches and old record players can all be taken apart and examined. Make sure there is always an adult around to supervise and to help if necessary.

Components also make great art. Maybe when they've finished checking out why the clock no longer works they might like to make a robot or a super machine artwork out of all the bits.

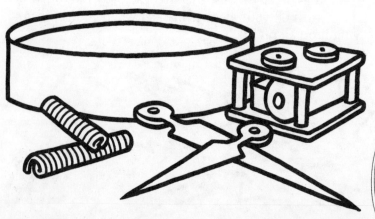

activity
291

WEATHER INFORMATION   10+

Encourage your older children's interest in the environment by helping them set up a weather station and recording and measuring each day's weather.

What You Need

- *Strong cardboard* • *2 broom handles*
- *Thermometer* • *Large tin*

What To Do

The weather station will need a rain gauge, a wind vane and a thermometer.

Attach the tin with suitable glue to the side or top of a broom handle and bury in the ground in an open part of the garden. Make sure it is firm enough not to be knocked over by strong winds. Your children will need a ruler to place in the tin to measure rainfall - a simple rain gauge.

To make the wind vane, you need a piece of strong cardboard about 15cm square. Mark each corner with the initials for the compass directions of North, South, East and West. Make a hole in the centre of the card so a broom handle fits in snugly and cut an arrow out of strong cardboard to attach to the top of the wind vane. Attach it so it will swing freely and point to the positions on the card. Bury it in the garden and use the early morning sun or a compass to make sure you have the correct positions.

Your children are then ready to begin measuring things like the amount of rainfall each month, the daily temperature, cloud formations, wind directions, and the amount of daylight hours.

Help them graph their findings. Their teacher will be most interested in this project also!

activity
292

BATS AND BALLS

2+ ✓

 ✓

Developing eye/hand co-ordination skills early will help your children's ability to play sports such as tennis, cricket, golf, softball and baseball when they are older.

 ✓

What You Need

• *Old pantihose* • *Wire coathangers*
• *Masking or insulating tape* • *Tennis ball*

 ✓

What To Do

Bend the coathanger into the shape of a racquet and straighten the bent handle. Re-bend the handle over so it is narrower and longer than before.

Cut one leg off the pantihose and keep for later. Pull the other leg over the racquet until taut, then wrap the rest of the pantihose around the handle. Cover with the tape until the handle is firm and easy to hold.

Put a tennis ball in the toe of the spare pantihose leg and tie from a tree branch, the clothes line, or a hook.

Your children will have lots of fun hitting the ball backwards and forwards. Make two bats so your children can hit with you or a friend or sibling. The bats are so soft they won't be hurt if they accidentally hit each other.

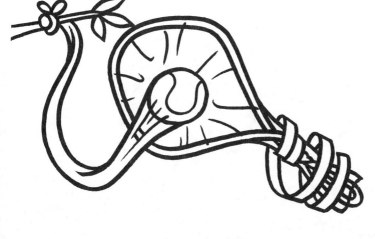

activity
293

FROZEN WATER PLAY

Great fun on a hot day.

2+

What You Need

- *Large container for water play*
- *Balloons of various shapes*
- *Food colouring • Eye droppers*

What To Do

Buy a packet of assorted shape balloons and select some different shapes. Fill each with water and place them in the freezer for a couple of days.

When they are frozen solid, cut away the balloon, leaving the frozen shape.

Place the iced shapes into your children's wading pool, large dish or even a baby bath. Your children will have lots of fun dropping food colouring onto the frozen shapes with the eye dropper and watching the colours change.

Another time you can fill plastic containers with coloured water for a different experience.

Your children will be fascinated by these colourful 'icebergs'.

activity

294

JUMPSCOTCH

2+ ✓

Younger children find traditional hopscotch too difficult. Develop their balance and co-ordination with simpler 'Jumpscotch'. (see Hopscotch - activity 305.)

 ✓

What You Need

- *Chalk to draw on pavers or concrete*
- *Stone or bean bag for throwing*

 ✓

What To Do

 ✓

Draw a pattern on the concrete, making sure the spaces are large enough for your children to jump in.

Show your children how to jump with their feet together from space to space until they reach the end of the jumpscotch. Show them how to turn around at the end and then jump back. When they have mastered this, play the game together using a stone or bean bag to throw.

You can vary the game by drawing different shapes (ovals, semi-circles, circles, squares, triangles and rectangles) and using their names. You could also draw the rectangles with just one foot shape in each so your children have to jump with their feet apart. Happy jumping!

activity
295

PAINT POTS

2+

A cheap, fun outdoor activity to do on a sunny day.

What You Need

- *Small bucket*
- *Elastic or cord*
- *Paint brush*
- *Food colouring*

What To Do

Young children love painting, but it is not always possible or practical to provide real paints. They also love painting with real brushes like Mum and Dad.

So, attach a real paint brush to an old empty paint tin or small bucket. Half fill the bucket with water and add some food colouring. Now they can 'paint' the paths, driveway, concrete, or even the outside of the house, and you can rest easy knowing it can all be hosed off later..!

activity
296

SPONGE TARGETS

2+

Lots of fun for the whole family on hot days.

What You Need

• *Sponge offcuts* • *Chalks* • *Bucket*

What To Do

Draw a clown's face or some other target on the brick walls of the house. Fill a bucket with water, dip the sponge pieces in the water and take it in turns to throw them at the target and 'wipe' it out. Great for a hot day as everyone gets nice and wet while you do it.

activity
297

TEDDY BEARS' PICNIC

2+

 ✓
 ✓
 ✓

 ✓

Next time you and your young children are having a bad day, arrange a Teddy Bears' Picnic with their favourite soft toys. They will be enchanted and you will be good friends again!

What You Need

- *Picnic food and drink*
- *Soft toys and, of course, your children's Teddy*

What To Do

Begin by making some simple invitations together. Decide with your children which 'toy friends' they would like to invite. They can decorate the invitations while you do the actual writing. Then they can be the 'postman' and deliver them.

Together, decide on the picnic fare - fruit, chunks of cheese, sausage and savoury biscuits, fairy bread make a simple but appealing picnic lunch. Don't forget cool drinks too!

Arrange it all on a rug or tablecloth in a cool part of the garden. A tea set adds to the fun also - your children will enjoy 'pouring' all their guests a drink.

Sing the 'Teddy Bears Picnic' song and read any books you have about bears together.

After the picnic is cleared away, pop your children into bed with all their cuddly friends for a nap and put your feet up. You deserve it!

activity **298**

WATER PLAY

2+ ✓

 ✓

Young children never tire of playing with water. Give your children lots of things to play with and they will be happily occupied for hours on a hot day. Remember, however, that young children must always be supervised near water.

 ✓

What You Need

- *Large container for water* • *A variety of plastic containers, measuring cups, plastic toys, large and small buckets, funnels, colanders, egg beater, plastic tubing, corks, tins with holes punched in them, sponges, PVC conduit and anything else you can think of!*

What To Do

Place your children's wading pool, baby bath or a large dish in a shady part of the garden on a hot day. Turn on the hose and let them fill the container (best if they are wearing their bathers!).

Provide lots of the above water play toys and they will have a great time.

For a change, add some food colouring to the water - this way they can see the water clearly as they pour and measure.

activity

299

WATER SLIDES

2+

If you have a grassy slope in your garden, turn it into a water slide and your children will have lots of fun sliding and cooling off.

What You Need

- *plastic sheeting or large strong plastic garbage bags*
- *plastic tent pegs*
- *sprinkler or hose*

What To Do

Use the plastic tent pegs to secure the plastic sheeting on a grassy incline in your garden. Set up the sprinkler or hose so the water runs down the plastic and the kids will have lots of fun splashing and sliding.

Adding a little detergent occasionnlly to the slide will increase the slipperyness but warn the children first. Don't forget to apply lots of sunscreen and to supervise this activity closely.

activity **300**

BEAN BAG BALANCING

4+

 ✓
 ✓
 ✓

 ✓
 ✓

Fun games to help develop your children's body co-ordination, balance and control.

What You Need

- *Bean bag for balancing*
- *Simple obstacle course using a tyre or hoop, cardboard boxes, beach towels or hessian bags, and a broom*

What To Do

Make an easy bean bag by filling a sock with lima beans, split peas or rice. Tuck the sock inside its mate so no filling can spill out.

Your children can help you mark out the obstacle course.

Think of lots of different ways together that they can carry the bean bag without using their hands - on their head, under their arm, jumping with it between their legs, under their chin, between their elbows and between their wrists.

They then choose a way to carry the bean bag from the start to the first object, then choose a different method, and so on until they have gone through the whole course. If they drop the bean bag at any stage, they go back to the start of that section and try again.

Have a turn yourself - it is not as easy as it sounds!

activity
301

FREEZE

4+

Another good outdoor game to play with a group of children.

What You Need

• *Space* • *A few players*

What To Do

One person is 'in' and stands, with their back to the other children, a fair distance away. The other children advance in a line towards the person who is 'in', who, every now and then turns around, and all the others have to instantly freeze. If any of these children are spotted moving, they are named by the person who is 'in' and must leave the game.

The first player to reach and touch the 'in' player is the winner and is 'in' for the next round.

activity
302

GARDEN OBSTACLE COURSES   4+

Make an obstacle course in the garden to help develop your children's balance and muscle control.

What You Need

- *Rope or the garden hose*
- *Rebounder or old mattress*
- *Cardboard boxes*
- *Strong smooth boards*

- *Ladder*
- *Tyres*
- *Hoops*
- *Broom*

What To Do

With your children, set up obstacle courses in the garden. Incorporate any structures you may have such as a slide or swings. Try to use as many different ways of moving as possible. Your children could try to:

Crawl under some garden chairs
Jump ten times on the rebounder or mattress
Jump through three or four tyres or hoops
Jump over the broom
Walk along the curvy rope or hose
Run around a tree
Crawl up a plank balanced on a strong box
Hop through the rungs of a ladder laid flat on the ground
Walk sideways back to the start

This game is as endless as your imaginations.

activity
303

HANKY TUGS

4+

A new way to play tug-of-war.

What You Need

- *Three players*
- *A rope tied together to make a circle*
- *Three hankies*

What To Do

The three players hold the rope at equal distances.
They then pull the rope tight. Place the hankies at equal distances
from each child. When you say 'Go', they must pull as hard as they
can on the rope with one hand to try to reach their hanky. The first
person to pick up their hanky is the winner.

activity
304

HOPSCOTCH

4+ ✓

*After your children have mastered Jumpscotch, playing Hopscotch will further develop their co-ordination and balance, and also help them learn numbers in a fun way. (see Jumpscotch - activity **295**)*

What You Need

- *Chalk to draw on pavers or concrete*
- *Stones or small bean bag to throw*

✓

✓

What To Do

Mark out a traditional hopscotch pattern or the one shown below on some concrete or pavers. Perhaps you and your children can come up with some new patterns of your own, maybe a rocketship hopscotch game?

Explain the rules of hopscotch to them. Throw the stone into section 1, jump over it and then hop in all sections up to 10. Do a jump-turn on 10, hop back again and then, while balancing on one leg in section 2, retrieve the stone. Next time, throw into section 2, then hop over that and so on. If one child throws a stone into the wrong section, it is the next player's turn.

Each player must remember which number they are up to for their next turn. Younger children can play by jumping rather than hopping on one leg.

activity

305

JUMPING ROPES

4+

Activities like these will help improve your children's co-ordination and balance.

What You Need

- *A length of rope*
- *Small cushion, bean bag or half a sock filled with dried beans*

What To Do

Tie a cushion or the bean bag/sock to the end of the rope. Swing the rope around just above the ground (not too fast at first!). Your children jump over the rope as it comes around.

This is fun to do with a few kids or other family members. When the rope hits someone they are out and the winner is the last one left in.

activity
306

KNOCK 'EMS

4+

Develop your children's throwing skills with a game of home-made 'Knock 'ems'.

What You Need

- *6 tins with lids (powdered milk or baby formula tins are ideal)*
- *Paint or collage materials for decorating the tins*
- *Sand or dirt* • *Balls or bean bags*

What To Do

Put some sand or dirt in the tins so they don't topple over too easily and replace the lids and tape closed.

Paint or decorate the tins with your children. Show them how to arrange the tins in a pyramid.

Throw the bean bags and count how many they knock down. Keeping the scores will be good counting practice too!

activity
307

NAILING FUN

4+

An activity that encourages the development of excellent eye-hand coordination.

What You Need

- *Small nails* • *Small tack hammer*
- *Piece of pine board about 25 cm square*
- *Threading material*

What To Do

If you are buying a piece of pine for this activity the above size is ideal but really any shape will be fine as long as it is large enough to work on. Timber furniture makers are always happy to let you have their pine off-cuts. Pine is ideal for hammering with young children because it is a soft timber.

Mark dots about 1-2 cms. apart around the outside of the board and your children can hammer a nail part of the way into each dot.

Then give them a selection of wool, string, elastic, raffia or perhaps even coloured wire to wind from nail to nail to make interesting patterns and shapes.

Another time you might like to mark the dots in the shape of a circle or perhaps a star to make a different pattern for your children to try.

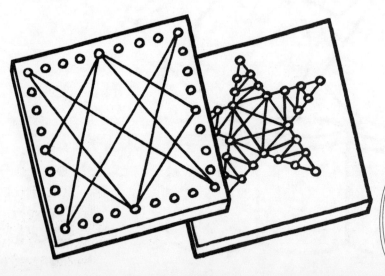

activity
308

PULLEYS

4+

Make a simple pulley with your children for lifting loads and playing rescue games with their teddies or dolls.

What You Need

- *Fishing line reel or large cotton reel*
- *Strong cord or string*
- *Two wire coat hangers or length of wire*
- *Pliers and wire cutters*

What To Do

Cut the wire coat hanger and, with the pliers, bend the wire through the reel (see the illustration) into the correct shape. Put the cord over the reel and tie a hook made from the second coat hanger hook onto the bottom.

Your children can use the pulley over the branch of a tree, from a cubby house, or even from the verandah.

They can use it for all sorts of games such as lifting lunch up into their cubby, lifting sand tools, or even playing 'Police Rescue' and lifting injured dolls or teddies.

To add to their interest, visit a building site together and watch cranes lifting their loads.

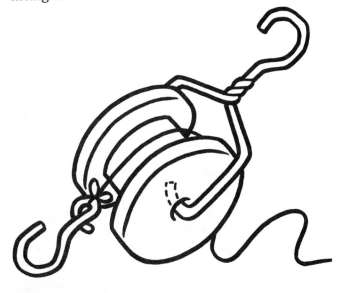

activity
309

ROPE FUN

4+ ✓

 ✓

 ✓

Use a length of rope to help your children develop their body control and co-ordination.

What You Need

 ✓

• *A long piece of rope*

 ✓

What To Do

Stretch out a long length of rope on the grass.
See if your children can think of lots of different ways
to move along it (your children should be barefooted).

They could try:

Walking along the rope
Walking backwards
Jumping from side to side along the rope
Doing bunny hops over the rope
Walking with one foot on either side of the rope without touching it
Hopping along the rope on one foot
Crawling along the rope
Moving along the rope using one hand and one foot

See if you can think of other ways of moving with your children.
After they have tried them with a straight rope, try them on a rope
that is laid in a wiggly line.

activity
310

TARGET PRACTICE

4+

Make some targets in the garden with your children and help improve their throwing skills.

What You Need

- *Wire coathanger or a child's plastic hoop*
- *String*
- *Balls or bean bags*

What To Do

Pull the coathanger into a round shape or use a hoop and lash it to a tree or the clothes line to make a stable target.

Your children will have lots of fun throwing balls or bean bags through the target.

To make it more interesting, tie balloons on strings or junk threadings to the target so they move when the children score a 'hit'.

As their aim improves, make them stand further away to increase the challenge.

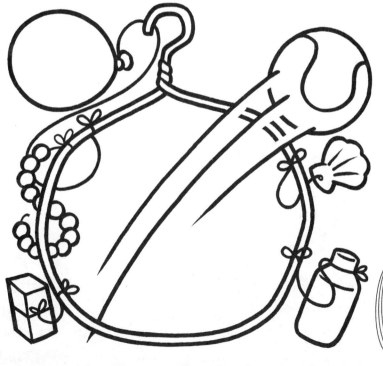

activity
311

WACKO

4+

A fun variation on a game of skittles.

What You Need

- *Empty plastic soft drink bottles*
- *Chalk*
- *Sand*
- *Large ball*

What To Do

Your children can help by pouring about a cup of sand into the bottom of each soft drink bottle so they don't topple easily.

Draw a large circle on the concrete or pavers with the chalk, or make a circle on the lawn with the hose.

Place all the bottles inside and take it in turns to roll a ball along the ground and see how many bottles you can each knock out of the circle.

Use this activity as a counting game as well and your children can keep the scores on paper or their blackboard.

activity

312

FLYING SAUCERS

6+

Make some exciting Flying Saucers to fly in the backyard with the children. See whose Flying Saucer will fly the greatest distance.

What You Need

- *Paper plates* • *Paper cups* • *Scissors*
- *Sticky tape or masking tape* • *Felt pens*

What To Do

Begin by helping the children cut the paper cups in half. Keep the bottom part and cut small slits along the top edge, and then bend them out to make flaps. Put the cup with the flaps down onto the paper plate and fasten with pieces of sticky tape or masking tape. Finally, help the children cut flaps around the outside of the plate. Fold each flap alternately forwards or backwards. These flaps will help the flying saucer fly.

Your children will enjoy using felt pens to draw windows and doors on their flying saucers, or buy a can of silver spray paint and spray them silver to look really hi-tech.

Go out at night sky-watching and see if you can really spot some alien visitors!

activity
313

FRENCH CRICKET

6+

A great family game that helps younger children learn some of the skills needed for playing conventional cricket later.

What You Need

- *A large soft plastic ball*
- *A small cricket bat, old tennis racquet or piece of wood shaped like a bat*

What To Do

Gather the family together to play a fast and furious game of French Cricket. One player holds the bat in front of their legs and the other players space themselves out in a large circle around that player. The object of the game is to try to hit the batsman's legs with the ball.

The batsman has to try to hit the ball away and is not allowed to move except when the ball has been hit and a player is running to fetch it. The batsman can then jump to another position. However, if the player fetching the ball sees this move, the batsman is out.

A fun family game!

activity
314

HOME-MADE QUOITS

6+

We always played quoits at Nanna's house when we were children. Help your own children make a set and improve their throwing skills.

What You Need

- *Empty plastic soft drink bottle*
- *Stones* • *Metal coat hangers*

What To Do

Put the stones into the soft drink bottle to stop it falling over and securely tape on the lid. To make the hoops, untwist the handle section of the coat hanger and retwist the wire to form circles. (If this is too hard on the fingers, cut off the handle with wire cutters and just use the rest).

Place the bottle on the ground and mark a spot for the children to throw from. (Older children will need a handicap!) Each player has ten throws at a time. Keep the scores and the person who hoops the most quoits over the bottle is the winner.

Quoits is a good game to play on a picnic or family gathering - even the older members of the family will love to have a go.

activity
315

PAPER PLANES

6+

Make some simple paper planes and have a competition with your children to see how far they can fly. If you have a house set on high ground have them fly their planes from the verandah top and watch which way the wind takes them.

What You Need

• *A4 paper*

What To Do

Fold a piece of A4 paper in half lengthways. Fold the top corner of the paper into the middle to form an arrow shape. Then fold it in again. Next, fold the 'wings' down on the sides to form the plane.

The wings can be closer in to make it like a high speed fighter jet, or sit further out to increase the aerobatics potential. You can staple along the body of the plane to make it stay in shape better. A paper clip attached to the nose will make it fly even faster!

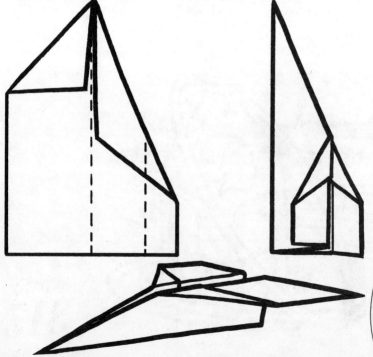

activity
316

PIGGY IN THE MIDDLE

6+

A game most of us have played in our youth!

What You Need

• *Three players* • *A ball*

What To Do

Stand two of the children about ten metres apart. The third child is 'Piggy' and, of course, stands in the middle.

'Piggy' has to try to catch the ball as the other two players throw it to each other. If the ball is dropped, any of the three can try to retrieve it. When 'Piggy' has managed to catch the ball, the person who was last to throw it becomes the new 'Piggy.'

activity
317

PUNCH BAG

6+

Next time your children are squabbling, make a punching bag with them so they can punch that instead of each other.

What You Need

- *Sugar bag (or sew a calico bag)*
- *Rope*
- *Filling such as newspaper, old rags, foam, dried grass*

What To Do

Your children can fill the bag with the selected filling. Tie a rope securely around the top of the bag and hang it from a beam or the branch of a tree.

A pair of boxing gloves would make a good birthday or Christmas gift to go with the punching bag.

Have a go yourself next time the children have stressed you out! It's better to punch the bag instead of yelling at them.

activity
318

SIMON SAYS

An oldie, but a goldie!

6+

What You Need

- *Players*
- *Space to play*

What To Do

Explain the rules to the children. You will give them instructions, but they can only do them if they hear 'Simon says'. So, if you say 'Run on the spot', they must remain still until the command 'Simon says, run on the spot!'

Players are eliminated if they do the wrong thing. The last player in is the winner and can give the commands next time.

activity

319

VOLLEYBALL

6+

Young children need lots of fun games with balls to develop ball skills for more formal ball games such as basketball and netball.

What You Need

• *A large soft plastic ball or balloon.*

What To Do

String up a net or simply a rope from between two trees at just above your child's head height. Bat and throw the ball back and forward to your child. Whoever fails to catch the ball must give a point to the other player.

This game is lots of fun played indoors also, but with a balloon instead of a ball. Simply clear space in a room and tie a string between the backs of two chairs. If you have more players add a few more balloons to increase the fun (and the challenge!).

activity
320

WHEELBARROW RACES

6+

Lots of fun to do and even more fun to watch.

What You Need

• *At least four children*

What To Do

Mark out a starting and finishing line for the wheelbarrow race. Divide the children into pairs. Each pair has to decide who is going to be the wheelbarrow first and who will be the pusher.

The 'wheelbarrow' gets down on his hands and his partner lifts him around the knees. Line them all up and begin the race.

Next time, swap over, so everyone has a turn at both roles.

Loads of laughs, but make sure you play it on soft grass.

activity
321

COIN TOSSING

Another good game that not only improves your children's throwing skills, but also gives them counting practice.

What You Need

- *Muffin tin*
- *Paper*
- *Pencil*
- *Coins*

What To Do

Cut out circles of paper to fit in the holes in the muffin tin. Give each hole a different number. Stand the tin against some books so it stands on an angle.

Mark a spot for the players to throw from and take it in turn to try to toss a coin into one of the holes in the muffin tin. Coins that land in a hole score that number of points.

Players must add up their own scores and keep a running total. The first player to reach a designated score (perhaps 100!) is the winner.

activity
322

DONKEY

8+

Most adults will remember this game from their own childhood. Play it again with your children and their friends.

What You Need

• *Children* • *Tennis ball*

What To Do

This was one of my favourite playground games at primary school, and the children of today will enjoy it too.

The children line up facing a wall - about two metres from it - except for the person who is 'it'. This person is the ball thrower - all the players will have a turn at this. The player with the ball throws the ball at the wall and, as it rebounds, everyone must jump over it. If a player is hit or touched by the ball they gain a letter, eventually spelling D O N K E Y !! The player is out when they get the whole word.

The winner of each game is the person who has the least number of letters when the game ends. (Time each game so everyone can have a turn at throwing). Keep a score sheet to see who is the overall winner.

activity
323

FIND THE BELL

8+

Listening games like this help children develop good listening habits in a fun play way.

What You Need

- *blindfolds (if you know a frequent traveller, ask them to collect some sleep-masks for you)*
- *a bell*
- *plenty of open space to play the game*

What To Do

Blindfold all the players except one. That person is 'it' and carries the bell. This must be rung all the time while the others try to catch the player with the bell, who must work very hard to stay out of the way of the other players.

Whoever tags that player has the next turn at ringing the bell.

activity
324

PARTY AND GROUP GAMES

ONE ELEPHANT WENT BALANCING   2+

A party game that 'littlies' will love to play.

What You Need

- *A group of small children*
- *A long piece of string or rope*

What To Do

If you know the tune, sing it for the children, otherwise teach it as a chant. Choose one child to be the first Elephant and the children do the choosing after that.

ONE ELEPHANT WENT BALANCING
FROM FOOT TO FOOT ON A PIECE OF STRING,
IT HAD SUCH ENORMOUS FUN
THAT IT CALLED FOR ANOTHER ELEPHANT TO COME.

The game continues until you decide that's enough on the string. The last verse goes like this:

FIVE ELEPHANTS WENT BALANCING
FROM FOOT TO FOOT ON A PIECE OF STRING,
ALL OF A SUDDEN THE PIECE OF STRING BROKE,
AND DOWN CAME ALL OF THE ELEPHANT FOLK!

Young children will, of course, love the last part where they all fall down on top of one another!

activity
325

RING A ROSY

2+

Younger children love this falling-down fun game.

What You Need

- *Children*
- *Room to play safely*
  - a good outside game on the grass

What To Do

All the children and adults hold hands and dance around singing:

RING A RING A ROSY
A POCKET FULL OF POSY
AH TISHOO AH TISHOO
WE ALL FALL DOWN

Then, sitting on the ground they can sing:

PICKING ALL THE DAISIES, THE DAISIES, THE DAISIES
PICKING ALL THE DAISIES
WE ALL JUMP UP!

Repeat a few times until everyone is exhausted!

activity
326

BIRD'S NEST GAME

4+

A fast and lively game to play with three or more children

What You Need

- *3 plastic hoops*
- *5 bean bags (fill old socks with sand, rice or dried beans to make quick and easy bean bags)*

What To Do

Explain to the children that the hoops are pretend birds' nests and that the bean bags are the eggs. Put the bean bags in the centre of the room and put the three hoops equidistant from them.

Choose three children to have the first turn - they each stand in their 'nest' or hoop. When you say "go" the children each run in, pick up a bean bag and run back and place it in their nest. They then run back for another one. When the bean bags have gone from the middle they can 'steal' them from each other's nests. When a child has three 'eggs' in their nest they sit down on them and yell 'Bird's Nest' and win the game. Remind the players that only one bean bag at a time can be placed in the nest and that they must be put in, not thrown from a distance.

This game is fast and furious and is just as funny for the onlookers as for the players. It moves so fast I often think it should be called 'perpetual motion'!

activity
327

BIRTHDAY PINATA

4+

Make a Mexican pinata with your children to use at their next birthday party.

What You Need

- *A balloon*
- *Newspaper and coloured paper*
- *Paint*
- *Wallpaper paste*
- *Streamers*
- *Lollies*

What To Do

Blow up the balloon if your children can't manage this, and then begin the papier mache process. Your children can help cut or tear the newspaper into strips.   Next, dip them in the glue and paste them over the balloon. Papier mache is best done over a few days to allow the layers to dry. Hang the balloon from the clothes line to dry really well.

When the papier mache is thick enough, burst the ballon and carefully cut a hole in the top.   Decorate it with colourful paints and bright patterns and hang streamers from the bottom. Fill with lollies.

At the party, hang up the pinata and the children take it in turns to hit it with a stick (blindfolds add an extra challenge) to break it so the lollies fall out. Lots of fun!

activity
328

DOGGIE, WHERE'S YOUR BONE? 4+

A game that children of all ages love to play.
All you need as a prop is a simple 'bone' cut out
of a plastic icecream lid or out of cardboard.

What You Need

• *Children* • *'Bone'* • *Blindfold*

What To Do

The children join hands to make a circle and then sit down.
Choose a child to have the first turn. This child sits in the middle of
the circle, wearing the blindfold and with the 'bone' behind their back.

Choose another child from the circle to creep out and steal the doggie's
'bone', hiding it behind their back.

Everyone then chants:

DOGGIE, DOGGIE, WHERE'S YOUR BONE?
SOMEBODY STOLE IT FROM YOUR HOME.
WHO STOLE THE BONE?

The child who stole the 'bone' replies:

"I STOLE THE BONE".

The blindfolded child then has to guess who has the bone. If the
children don't know each other well enough to name, they can point at
who they think has the bone. The game is harder if you encourage the
children not to tell who has the bone, not to giggle if they have it and
everyone puts their hands behind their back - not just the person with
the bone.

activity
329

HEY, MR. CROCODILE!

4+

A good game to play at a children's party or any time a group of kids is together.

What You Need

• *Children*

What To Do

Choose one child to be Mr. Crocodile or play it yourself for a while if the children are not familiar with the game. The rest of the children line up on the other side of an imaginary river. They then begin asking Mr. Crocodile if they can cross the river. Mr. Crocodile replies 'Yes', but with a condition.

HEY, MR. CROCODILE, CAN WE CROSS THE WATER
TO SEE YOUR LOVELY DAUGHTER
FLOATING IN THE WATER
LIKE A CUP AND SAUCER.

Mr. Crocodile replies:

YES, IF YOU'RE WEARING RED! (or shoes, buttons, hair ribbons, etc.).

A fun game that helps young children discriminate and use language well.

activity
330

I WROTE A LETTER

4+

I'm sure nearly everyone has played this game at birthday parties, but here it is to refresh your memories. Provide a handkerchief for the 'letter', or an envelope if you wish.

What You Need

• *Children* • *Handkerchief or envelope*

What To Do

The children join hands to make a circle and then sit down. Choose a child to have the first turn. The child walks around the circle with the hanky while everyone chants or sings:

I WROTE A LETTER TO MY LOVE
AND ON THE WAY I DROPPED IT
SOMEONE MUST HAVE PICKED IT UP
AND PUT IT IN THEIR POCKET
IT'S YOU! IT'S YOU! IT'S Y O U!

At the end the child drops the hanky behind another child's back. When that child realises it's behind their back, they jump up and chase the first child around the circle. The first child must run to the empty place and sit down before they are tagged.

The child who was chasing then has the next turn.

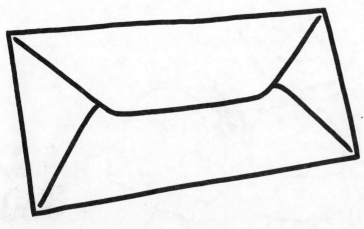

activity
331

LITTLE TOMMY TITTLEMOUSE   4+

A game to play at a children's party or just with a group of children.

What You Need

• *Children*

What To Do

The children join hands to make a circle and then sit down. Choose a child to have the first turn at being 'it' in the middle of the circle, closing their eyes. Choose another child to be the first to have their voice identified. The children in the circle then chant:

LITTLE TOMMY TITTLEMOUSE
SAT INSIDE HIS LITTLE HOUSE
SOMEONE'S KNOCKING, ME OH MY,
SOMEONE'S CALLING 'IT IS I'!

Only the child picked to have their voice identified says the 'IT IS I'. The child in the circle has to try to identify it. Then that child has a turn at being 'Tommy Tittlemouse'.

activity
332

MR. BEAR

4+

Another group game to play with a few children or at a birthday party.

What You Need

- *Children*
- *Something to be the honey pot*

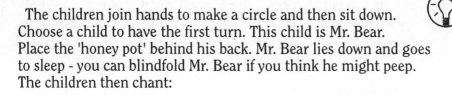

What To Do

The children join hands to make a circle and then sit down. Choose a child to have the first turn. This child is Mr. Bear. Place the 'honey pot' behind his back. Mr. Bear lies down and goes to sleep - you can blindfold Mr. Bear if you think he might peep. The children then chant:

ISN'T IT FUNNY HOW BEARS LIKE HONEY!
GO TO SLEEP MR. BEAR!

Choose a child, who then creeps out and steals the 'honey pot'. When the child has returned to his space in the circle and put the 'honey pot' behind his back, he says:

WAKE UP MR. BEAR!

Mr. Bear then has to try and guess who has the 'honey pot'. When he has guessed, the child with the 'honey pot' becomes the next Mr. Bear. Make some honey sandwiches to have after the game and perhaps a quick Winnie the Pooh story might be in order.

activity
333

OLD MOTHER WITCH

4+

An old group game which will be a popular party game or a great Halloween night game.

What You Need

• *Children*

What To Do

The children join hands to make a circle and then sit down. Choose a child to have the first turn. The child walks around the inside of the circle while the other children chant:

OLD MOTHER WITCH COULDN'T FIND HER STITCH
RODE HER BROOMSTICK ROUND AND ROUND
THEN ASKED ANOTHER FRIEND TO TOWN
WHOOSH, WHOOSH, WHOOSH, WHOOSH, WHAM!

On 'Wham' the child points their arm like a witch's wand at another child and that child then becomes Old Mother Witch!

activity
334

ORANGES AND LEMONS

4+

An oldie but a goldie! A game most of us have played at birthday parties when we were young. Teach it to your children at their parties and it will be just as popular today as it was then.

What You Need

• *Children*

What To Do

Choose two taller children to form an archway with their hands. They then decide with an adult which one is going to be the Orange and which the Lemon. The other children make a line behind a leader. They then walk through the archway chanting:

ORANGES AND LEMONS SAY THE BELLS OF ST. CLEMENTS
YOU OWE ME FIVE FARTHINGS SAY THE BELLS OF ST. MARTINS
WHEN WILL YOU PAY ME SAY THE BELLS OF OLD BAILEY?
WHEN I GROW RICH SAY THE BELLS OF SHOREDITCH
HERE COMES A CANDLE TO LIGHT YOU TO BED
HERE COMES A CHOPPER TO CHOP OFF YOUR - YOUR - YOUR - YOUR - YOUR - HEAD!

On the final head the archway is lowered and a child is caught. The archway children then take the 'caught' child away and ask them if they want to be an Orange or a Lemon (keep it a secret which child is which). When they have chosen, they line up behind that archway child. When all the children have been caught in the archway and have chosen to be an Orange or a Lemon, they form two teams and have a Tug-of-War!

activity

335

POSSUMS IN THE TREE

4+

A fast-moving game to play in the backyard with a group of children. A great party game too.

What You Need

- *Lots of children*
- *Space to run*

What To Do

Divide the children into groups of three. Two children in each group become the tree by placing their hands on each other's shoulders, thus forming a tree with a hollow in the middle. The third child in each trio becomes the possum in the tree (standing between the 'tree').

Keep a few children out as extra possums who don't have a tree. When you clap or whistle, all the possums have to run to a new 'tree', giving the extra possums a chance to capture a tree.

Make sure all the children have a turn at being the possums as well as the trees.

activity
336

SARDINES

4+

A very funny game that is just right to play at family gatherings or with a large group of children.

What You Need

• *A house with lots of hiding places*

What To Do

One person is chosen to be the 'SARDINE', and then goes to hide while the rest of the players close their eyes and count to 100. They then go and look for the 'SARDINE'.

When the 'SARDINE' is found by someone, that person must squeeze into the 'SARDINE'S' hiding place with the 'SARDINE'. (Don't forget to remind the players before they start to keep as quiet as possible while they are hiding - giggling is a real give-away!) As each player finds the 'SARDINE', they must squeeze into the same hiding place. Finally, everyone is there - squeezed in like a tin of sardines!

The person who found the 'SARDINE' first, becomes the next 'SARDINE'.

activity
337

THE FARMER IN THE DELL   4+

A traditional game that children always love to play at a party or a group gathering.

What You Need

• *Lots of children*

What To Do

Begin by standing the children in a circle and choose a 'farmer' to stand in the middle. The song begins. As each new character is introduced, choose a child to play that role in the middle of the circle.

THE ARMER IN THE DELL, THE FARMER IN THE DELL
HI HO THE DAIRY-O THE FARMER IN THE DELL.
THE FARMER TAKES A WIFE, THE FARMER TAKES A WIFE,
HI HO THE DAIRY-O THE FARMER TAKES A WIFE.

The song continues:

THE WIFE TAKES A CHILD etc
THE CHILD TAKES A NURSE etc
THE NURSE TAKES A DOG etc
THE DOG TAKES A CAT etc
THE CAT TAKES A MOUSE etc
THE MOUSE TAKES SOME CHEESE etc
WE ALL EAT THE CHEESE etc

Don't choose a timid child for the cheese or they may not enjoy being eaten!

activity
338

THREE-LEGGED RACES

4+

An old Sunday School picnic favourite from my childhood.

What You Need

- *Old pantihose or scarves*
- *At least four children*

What To Do

Mark out a starting and finishing line first.

The children divide into pairs. Make sure they remove their shoes, and then tie each pair of children firmly together around their ankles with a scarf or old pantihose. They then hold each other around the waist.

Line up all the contestants and begin the race. If the children are having difficulties, remind them to start walking by moving their joined legs together first. Speed is not essential at first - it's more important to get a rhythm going.

Give them lots of practice until everyone gets the hang of it!

activity
339

TREASURE HUNT

4+

A fun party game for the small fry.

What You Need

• *lots of players*
• *some treasure - perhaps a coin*

What To Do

Choose one child to be the first 'treasure hunter'.
All the others sit in a circle on the floor with the treasure hunter
in the middle of the circle. The players pass the 'treasure' around
the circle from hand to hand and the 'treasure hunter' has to point to
who has the treasure. Encourage the children to make it harder by all
pretending to pass the 'treasure' even if they're not.

The 'treasure hunter' only has three guesses as this keeps the game
moving and means everyone has a turn. (Young children find it difficult
to wait for their turn.) The person with the treasure becomes the next
'treasure hunter'.

activity
340

WHAT'S THE TIME, MR WOLF? 4+

A great party game.

What You Need

• *Lots of space* • *Lots of players*

What To Do

One child is 'Mr Wolf' and stands a fair distance away with their back to the other children. The other children hold hands and advance in a line, step by step, as they chant, 'What's the time, Mr Wolf?' They then stop walking. After each question Mr Wolf turns around and says a time, e.g. '7 o'clock'. Finally, when they are very close, Mr Wolf turns and says 'Dinner Time!'

The children turn and run away as fast as they can with 'Mr Wolf' chasing them. When someone is caught, they are the next 'Mr Wolf'.

activity
341

WHO STOLE THE COOKIE?

4+

A fun party game to play with a group of children.

What You Need

• *A group of children*

What To Do

Sit the children in a circle for this game so everyone can see each other. Start the rhythm of the game by doing one clap of hands and then a knee tap. CLAP TAP CLAP TAP. When the children are all following the rhythm, teach them the chant:

WHO STOLE THE COOKIE FROM THE COOKIE JAR?
TOM STOLE THE COOKIE FROM THE COOKIE JAR.
Tom then says,
WHO ME?
The group responds with:
YES YOU!
Tom then says:
COULDN'T BE!
The group then says:
THEN WHO?
Tom then chooses the next player:
ANDREW!
The game continues:
WHO STOLE THE COOKIE FROM THE COOKIE JAR?
ANDREW STOLE THE COOKIE FROM THE COOKIE JAR.

A great game, which also develops children's memory and verbal skills.

activity
342

NOISY ANIMAL PAIRS

6+

 ✓
 ✓
 ✓
 ✓
✓
✓

A noisy, funny game to play at a party or with a group of children.

What You Need

• *An even number of players* • *Pieces of paper*
• *A cardboard box or container*

What To Do

Divide the number of children by two and think of that many animals. They must be animals that all the players are familiar with, and know what sounds they make.   Write the name of each animal on two pieces of paper. Place all the animal names in a box and the children take it in turn to draw out a name. (They must keep this a secret.)

Now the game begins. The children pretend to be the animal they have drawn out and they must make the noise that animal makes. At the same time, however, they must also listen to the others to find the child who is making the same noise as themselves. The first animal pair to find each other are the winners, but the game continues until everyone has found their pair.

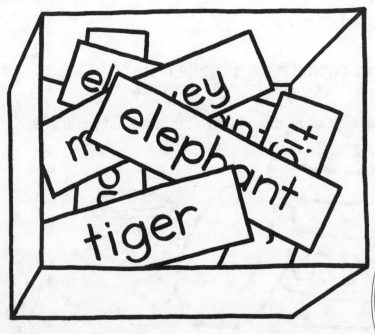

activity
343

STATUES

6+

A good game for a party or play it any time you have a group of children to keep occupied.

What You Need

• *music - a cassette or C.D. player or the radio*

What To Do

The players spread out. When the music starts they begin dancing around the room. Suddenly stop the music and everyone has to 'freeze' in whatever position they were in. Watch the children carefully and the first person to move is out.

The game continues until only one person is left, who is the winner.

activity
344

PARTNERS

8+

An excellent ice-breaker to play at a party, or fun to play with the family.

What You Need

- *An even number of players*
- *Pieces of card* • *A pencil or pen*

What To Do

Put on your thinking cap and try to think of as many things that go together as you can. Here are some to get you going:

- Adam and Eve
- Knife and fork
- Bacon and eggs
- Hide and seek
- Bat and ball
- Night and day
- Batman and Robin
- Spaghetti and meatballs
- Bread and butter
- Soap and water
- Cup and saucer
- Jack and Jill
- Cats and dogs
- Hansel and Gretel

I am sure you will be able to think of lots more. Write down half of each pair on one piece of card and its pair on the other. Shuffle up the cards and deal them out.   Each player receives a card. The players then go round the room trying to find their partners (and meeting everyone else as they go).

The first pair to find their mate are the winners, but the game continues until everyone is matched.

Then do some brainstorming to think of other things that go together.

activity
345

WHO IS IT?

8+

A good game to play at a party.

What You Need

- *A baby photo of each child coming to the party (obtain them secretly from the children's parents beforehand)*
- *Pencils and sheets of paper*

What To Do

Pin or Blu-Tack up the baby photos and number each one. Give each child a piece of paper with a list of all the children who are at the party on each one.

The children then wander around looking at the photos (and probably at each other) until they have written a number beside each name.

Have a time limit on the game and then see who has the most right. Have an appropriately funny prize for this game - perhaps a big tin of baby powder or a big baby's dummy!

activity
346

GUESS WHO?

10+

A family game to play together or use it as a game at a child's birthday party.

What You Need

• *Pieces of paper*
• *Sticky or masking tape or safety pins*

What To Do

Before you begin the game, write the names of several famous people on the slips of papee. Choose one person to have the first turn and pin a famous name on their back. They then have to try to discover who they are by asking questions like - 'Am I a female?' 'Do I star in movies?' 'Am I Australian?' 'Was I born in England?' and so on.

They can only receive YES or NO answers and they can only ask each person one question before they ask someone else.

At the end of the game, the player who discovered the identity of the famous person with the least number of questions is the winner.

activity
347

AUSTRALIA DAY

4+

 ✓

Help your children learn more about our special Australian customs and traditions.

 ✓

 ✓

What You Need

- *Green and yellow crepe paper*
- *Gum branches* • *Australia Day food*

What To Do

 ✓

The 26th of January is Australia Day commemorating the day in 1788 when the First Fleet landed in Sydney Cove. It is now an Australian holiday and most towns and cities have Australia Day picnics or celebrations. Why not go to one with the family or have an Australia Day party at home.

Your children can help you make green and yellow streamers and gather gum branches to decorate the barbecue area.

Serve traditional bush fare for the barbie; maybe barbecued chops, sausages and damper followed by pavlova and a good strong cup of billy tea. If you want to be more adventurous, many Aussie bush foods are now available in delis and specialty shops. After lunch have some competitions such as horseshoe throwing or a tug of war. Maybe you could have a sing-song with songs like Waltzing Matilda or the Wild Colonial Boy, or if someone is good at reading poetry, find an anthology of Banjo Patterson's - great Aussie entertainment!

activity

348

AUSTRALIA DAY DAMPER

4+

 ✓
 ✓
 ✓

 ✓
 ✓

Go for a picnic in the bush on Australia Day and make billy tea and damper like the pioneers. Begin a great family tradition this year.

What You Need

Ingredients:
- *4 cups self-raising flour*
- *30 grams butter*
- *1 cup milk*
- *1 teaspoon salt*
- *1/2 cup water*

What To Do

Sift the flour and salt into a mixing bowl. Cut the butter into small pieces and show your children how to rub them in with their fingers.

Let your children measure the milk and water and add to the bowl. Mix it all together with the knife.

Let them knead the dough on the floured board (don't forget to flour their hands too!).

Shape it into a damper shape and cut a cross in the top.

Cook in a well greased camp oven in the coals or on a baking tray in a moderate oven for about half-an-hour.

Yummy with golden syrup, honey, jam or just butter!

activity
349

CHRISTMAS PAPER CHAINS   4+

Decorate the house for Christmas or a special occasion with old-fashioned paper chains. They not only look festive, but they are a fun way for your children to improve their cutting skills and learn how to use a stapler.

What You Need

- *Scrap paper (old Christmas wrapping looks bright)*
- *Scissors* • *Stapler* • *Ruler*

What To Do

Help your children use their ruler to mark out lengths of paper about 5 cm wide. Cut out the strips, and then they can cut each long strip into 20 cm lengths.

Take the first piece and fold it over to form a loop and then staple. Remind them to always use the stapler flat on a table and to press it down hard with both hands until they hear two clicks. Learning to staple needs quite a lot of hand strength, so help them practice and be patient!

Next, they put another piece of paper through the loop and staple, and so on until the chain is as long as you need or as long as their interest lasts!

Hang them up together and admire their hard work.

activity
350

CHRISTMAS TWIG TREE

4+

Go for a bush walk with your children and collect lots of twigs to make a different sort of Christmas tree.

What You Need

- *Milk carton (cut in half - use the bottom section)*
- *Quick set plaster (available from hardware stores)*
- *Hessian or Christmas fabric*
- *Ribbon* • *Twigs*

What To Do

Arrange lots of twigs so they form a balanced shape in the milk carton. Carefully pour in the plaster and allow to set. Wrap the Christmas fabric or hessian around the milk carton and tie with a decorative contrasting bow.

Your children will have lots of fun helping and then decorating your different Christmas tree. It looks great 'au natural' but it can also be sprayed with gold or silver paint for a very pretty effect.

activity
351

FATHER'S DAY BOTTLES

4+

Teach your children the pleasure of giving by making a special gift for someone they love.

What You Need

- *An attractive glass jar*
- *Glass paints (available at craft shops)*
- *Fine brushes or cotton buds* • *Goodies to go in it*

What To Do

I think that the gifts that children make for parents both at home and at school, pre-school or kindy are infinitely more precious to a parent than a bought gift. Help your children make a special gift for Dad for Father's Day.

If you have an interesting glass jar, use that (Moccona coffee jars are nice) or else visit your local 'junk' shop - they often sell nice chunky glass jars with large cork lids for a couple of dollars.

Buy some bright pots of 'Glossies' glass paint from your local craft shop. By using this special paint the jar can be washed and the design isn't lost in the sink.

Your children paint on the design, then follow the directions carefully on your brand of paint for firing in the oven.

When the bottle is cool, fill with Dad's favourite goodies - my son filled his with my husband's favourite 'Fantail' lollies but at pre-school we made spicy 'Nuts & Bolts' and used that!

Grandpas might appreciate a bottle as a gift also.

activity
352

HOLIDAY SCRAPBOOK

4+

 ✓
 ✓
 ✓
 ✓
 ✓

A great way to keep family holiday memories alive.

What You Need

- *Scrapbook*
- *Glue*
- *Photos and holiday mementos*
- *Drawing and writing materials*

What To Do

While you are on holidays, save all the memorabilia, such as train tickets, fun park entries, postcards and photos. (When you have your holiday snaps developed, have doubles made - one set for your children's holiday scrapbook and the other set for the family photo album).

Assemble all the mementos and photos (pick a rainy day to do this) and glue them in the scrapbook in chronological order - a good memory activity. Encourage your children also to draw some pictures about the holiday in the scrapbook. Your older children can write the sub-titles, younger children tell you and you do the writing.

Older children can write a story about the best thing they did on holidays, while younger children can dictate their story for you to write. You may be surprised - our child recently spent a night in a small country hospital on holidays after a fall and that still rates as the best part of the holiday!

activity
353

LETTERS TO SANTA

4+

Help your children write a letter to Santa Claus and post it together. Write a reply and send it back to them so they have the excitement of receiving a letter also.

What You Need

- *Paper* • *Pencils and drawing pens*
- *Envelope* • *Stamp*

What To Do

Talk about Santa with your young children. Tell them that Santa would love to hear all about them. They can draw pictures of themselves, the family and your home. Your children can tell you what to write.

Next, they might like to draw or cut out from toy catalogues the things they might like from Santa. I always stress to my son that Santa can only bring one large present and fill his stocking as he has lots of children to deliver to and we must share.

Finally, address the letter together. Your children can stick on the stamp, and then together you can go for a walk to the mail box to post it.

Make sure the reply comes in a few days as young children find it very difficult to wait for special things!

Dear Santa,
I hope you are well.
I have been a good girl. Yesterday I helped my mum clean my room. I have written a list of things I want for Christmas on the next page.
Love
xxx
Sarah

A bike
doll

activity
354

SAINT VALENTINE'S DAY

4+

February 14th is traditionally the day for lovers. Make a Valentine's card with your children for them to give to someone special.

What You Need

- *Cardboard - pink or red look great*
- *Strong glue such as Aquadhere*
- *Decorations such as ribbon, lace, pretty stickers*
- *Flowers from the garden*

What To Do

Draw some hearts on the cardboard and your children can cut them out. Let them use their own imagination to decorate them. Help younger children write on the back of their heart, older children can do their own.

Your children may like to write their name, but traditionally Valentine cards are anonymous! Deliver the Valentines together!

activity
355

CHRISTMAS PASTA DECORATIONS 6+

Pasta glued onto cardboard makes cheap, but decorative, Christmas decorations. Make some with your children this Christmas.

What You Need

- *Pasta of different shapes and sizes*
- *Cardboard*
- *Can of gold spray paint*
- *String or gold ribbon*
- *PVA Glue*

What To Do

Cut the cardboard into small shapes - circles, rectangles and squares - with your children. Then punch a hole in each to tie it on the Christmas tree. They then glue an assortment of different pasta shapes onto the cardboard. They look great glued on both sides, so wait until one side is completely dry and then they can glue some on the other side.

When they have made enough, take them outside and carefully spray them with the gold spray paint (definitely an adult job).

When the paint has dried, thread some gold ribbon or Christmas tie through the holes and hang them on the tree. Wait for the compliments!

activity
356

CHRISTMAS SCENTED PINE CONES 6+

Make some attractive scented pine cones together to decorate your home at Christmas, or give some away as special gifts.

What You Need

- *Pine cones*
- *Cloves*
- *Red or green crepe paper or fabric*
- *Scissors*
- *Red or green ribbon*
- *Thumb tacks or craft glue*

What To Do

Show your children how to wrap each clove in a tiny piece of the crepe paper or fabric and insert in the pine cones (do this part carefully because some pine cones are quite prickly!). When all the holes are filled, help them attach a length of red, green or 'Christmassy' ribbon to hang it by. The ribbon can be glued to the top of the pine cone with strong craft glue, or attached with a tack.

They look lovely hanging from the tree, or hang several with different length ribbons together from a curtain track.

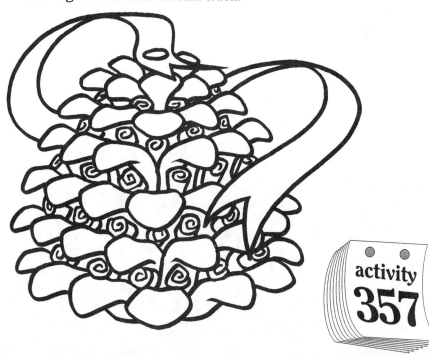

activity
357

CHRISTMAS SNOWFLAKES

6+

Use up scraps of gold, silver and Christmas paper by making pretty Christmas snowflakes with your children.

What You Need

• *Coloured paper* • *Scissors* • *Ribbon* • *Blu-Tack*

What To Do

Help your children cut up the scraps of paper into different sized squares. Next, they fold the paper square into a triangle and then fold it again. They then cut out notches along the edges with their scissors. When they open out the paper they will have beautiful snowflakes.

Hang them with coloured wrapping ribbon and attach them to the ceiling with small blobs of Blu-Tack.

They will look pretty and festive hanging above your Christmas tree or twirling in front of an open window.

activity
358

CHRISTMAS WRAPPING PAPER 6+

Save money and have fun too by making your own individual Christmas wrapping paper with your children.

What You Need

- *Red and green paint (acrylic paint works best and is available from toy or art & craft shops)*
- *Two kitchen sponges*
- *Two plastic plates or polystyrene trays*
- *Potatoes • Sharp knife*
- *Glitter • Newsprint paper*

What To Do

Place the kitchen sponges on the plates and pour a little green paint on one and red on the other. Spread the paint thickly across the sponges.

Next, cut some large potatoes in half and carefully cut some simple Christmas shapes out of them with a sharp knife. The shapes must stick out at least 2 cm above the rest of the potato half. Stars, bells, Christmas trees or a candy cane all look effective.

Your children press the potato onto the paint then print with it on the newsprint. While the paint is still wet, sprinkle a little gold or silver glitter on to add a festive touch.

Your Christmas gifts will look wonderful wrapped in your children's art work.

activity
359

NEW YEAR RESOLUTIONS   6+

Teach your children some traditions to see in the New Year and encourage them to begin something new - maybe keep their room tidier or pick up their toys without being nagged by Mum or Dad!

What You Need

• *Time together*

What To Do

Do some reading about New Year traditions and discuss them with your children. The Scots celebrate New Year in a big way with their Hogmanay festival and the Chinese New Year (which occurs later in January to mid-February) is a great festival to be part of. If you have a Chinatown near where you live, there is usually a procession, or take your children to a Chinese restaurant for lunch to sample some yummy Yum Cha.

Together plan some New Year resolutions and make a list. Involve the rest of the family too! Check your lists again in March and see how everyone is going. Perhaps you could make some family resolutions too, like making Sundays a family day where you try to do something special together.

activity
360

SAINT PATRICK'S DAY

6+

Celebrate the 17th March, St. Patrick's Day, with your children.

What You Need

• *Irish songs* • *Irish stories* • *Green food*

What To Do

Explain to your children who St. Patrick was. Many Australian families have links with Ireland. If yours does, see if you have any photos you can look at together of your Irish ancestors. Find Ireland in the atlas or go to the library and borrow some books about Ireland.

Finally, cook some Irish stew for tea with your children and serve it with green mashed potatoes and green cordial!

activity
361

SHROVE TUESDAY PANCAKES 6+

Shrove Tuesday is the Tuesday just before Lent begins. Lent is the period of forty days before Easter and is a time of fasting. Make some pancakes together with your children for breakfast or dessert on Shrove Tuesday (Pancake Tuesday).

What You Need

Ingredients:
- *1 cup sifted plain flour*
- *1 egg*
- *1 cup milk*
- *Pinch salt*
- *Butter for cooking*

Utensils:
- *Whisk*
- *Mixing bowl or jug*
- *Measuring cup*
- *Crepe pan*
- *Spatula*

What To Do

Your children can help you collect the ingredients. Beat the egg and stir in the flour and salt. Gradually add the milk to the mixture and stir until it is smooth.

I prefer to make pancakes in a jug as it is easier to pour the mixture into a pan. Melt a small amount of butter in the crepe pan and pour in enough mixture to cover the base of the pan.

Turn once. We love pancakes with lemon juice and castor sugar or strawberries in our family. You will probably have your own favourite topping.

activity
362

ANZAC DAY

8+ ✓

 ✓

What To Do

Many children come home from school puzzled and concerned because of talk about war at school before Anzac Day or Remembrance Day.

Explain to your children the history of the World Wars, perhaps using an atlas to show where the distant countries are in the world.

Explain the significance of the word Anzac (Australian and New Zealand Army Corps) and about Gallipoli. Tell them why veterans still march on Anzac Day and the meaning of Remembrance Day. (The first World War finished in 1918 on the 11th hour of the 11th day of the 11th month).

Perhaps some older relations have some medals or other war memorabilia to look at or old photos. Take your children to an Anzac parade or a dawn wreath laying ceremony.

Older children may enjoy watching a video such as 'Gallipoli' with you.

activity
363

CHRISTMAS NEWSPAPER

8+

A great way to keep in touch with distant family and friends at Christmas time.

What You Need

• *Family photos*
• *Family news*

What To Do

Suggest to your children a few weeks before Christmas that they could help you make a family newspaper to be sent to family and friends with the Christmas cards.

They can be the 'reporters' gathering news and interesting items from the rest of the family. They might like to try their hand at drawing some cartoons or pictures to include in it.

If you have a computer and printer, printing it out will be simple. If not, collate it and take it to your nearest photocopying shop.

Lots of fun and the folks you send it to will love receiving it.

activity
364

EASTER CANDLE CARVING 10+

A simple, but most effective decoration for your older children to make for Easter.

 ✓

 ✓

What You Need

 ✓

- *White wax candles* • *Small sharp knife*
- *Sharp pencil* • *Acrylic paint* • *Rags*

 ✓

What To Do

 ✓

Your children warm a candle by rubbing it between their hands. Next, they carefully scratch a pattern onto the candle with the pencil and, using the knife, they carve out the pattern.

 ✓

When that is finished, they polish the candle with a soft rag and then rub the candle surface with some acrylic paint, making sure the paint goes into the carved surface.

When the paint is dry they polish it again with a soft cloth.

Group the candles together for a decorative effect and light them for Easter lunch.

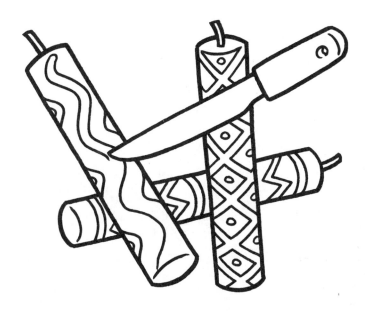

activity

365

ALPHABETICAL INDEX

ALPHABETICAL INDEX

ALPHABETICAL INDEX

ALPHABETICAL INDEX

ALPHABETICAL INDEX

MY OWN ACTIVITIES

MY OWN ACTIVITIES

MY OWN ACTIVITIES

MY OWN ACTIVITIES

MY OWN ACTIVITIES

MY OWN ACTIVITIES

MY OWN ACTIVITIES

MY OWN ACTIVITIES

MY OWN ACTIVITIES

MY OWN ACTIVITIES